What people are saying about

The First Sisters: Lilith and Eve

Lady Ashton has written a book worthy of attention. A timely study that places a new look at the women in civilization and society around the world rising to equality. Lady and I have shared our magick to benefit of equal power in the balance between woman and man. We have empowered ourselves from the history of priestesses that have come before us.

Laurie Cabot, HP

Pagan Portals

The First Sisters: Lilith and Eve

Pagan Portals
The First Sisters: Lilith and Eve

Lady Haight-Ashton

Winchester, UK
Washington, USA

First published by Moon Books, 2019
Moon Books is an imprint of John Hunt Publishing Ltd., No. 3 East Street, Alresford
Hampshire SO24 9EE, UK
office1@jhpbooks.net
www.johnhuntpublishing.com
www.moon-books.net

For distributor details and how to order please visit the 'Ordering' section on our website.

Text copyright: Lady Haight-Ashton 2018

ISBN: 978 1 78904 079 1
978 1 78904 080 7 (ebook)
Library of Congress Control Number: 2018936951

A CIP catalogue record for this book is available from the British Library.

Design: Stuart Davies

Printed and bound by CPI Group (UK) Ltd, Croydon, CR0 4YY, UK
US: Printed and bound by Edwards Brothers Malloy 15200 NBN Way #B, Blue Ridge Summit,
PA 17214, USA

We operate a distinctive and ethical publishing philosophy in all areas of our business, from our global network of authors to production and worldwide distribution.

Contents

Foreword

In Lady Haight-Ashton's compelling historical and personal revisiting of the ancient fable of Lilith, the first created female, and her relationship with her younger sister, Eve, and the first created male known as Adam, the reader is carefully guided to tread the path of " What if? "

It has often been said that history is written by the winners. Those of us familiar with the "Herstory" of Spirituality of the Sacred Feminine are well aware of this propaganda ploy. Rather than acknowledging females as "real-life symbols of the Great Goddess, the Primordial Mother of all," as did pre biblical cultures, patriarchal-dominated religious dogma has for millennia continued to create, whether substantiated by fact or motivated by political advantage and power, ideological narratives portraying archetypal females: Goddesses, heroines, mothers or mystics, as of less status and worthy of less veneration than males.

Whether one believes that the Bible and its creation story of exactly what occurred and how it occurred in the Garden of Eden so long ago is myth or the literal word of God, Lady's well-researched work offers us a glimpse into the impact on the human psyche that this potent scenario made in ancient JudeoChristian times, and thus the balance – or imbalance – of power between female and male that continues even in today's world.

Lady asks us to consider: Was the old biblical story, changed or misinterpreted in translation, or purposely created as a tool to transform the ancient matriarchal belief system to dominate rather than venerate womanhood? By "demonizing" Lilith and making Eve (already not so subtly portrayed as less equal to Adam) the perpetrator of "original sin" in this widely circulated creation story, women in many cultures worldwide were disempowered and the destiny of womankind altered.

In reading *The First Sisters: Lilith and Eve*, we join Lady and all Goddess believers on this "Herstoric" journey to bring the Goddess back!

Blessed Be With Love From Salem,

Rev. Amy "Gypsy" Ravish HPs. WQ, Writer, entrepreneur, ritualist, recording artist

Preface

As a Sacred Dancer and choreographer, I was always fascinated with ancient Goddess mythologies. My eyes opened to many tales but the one that held me fast was that of Lilith. Then unexpectedly I received a visit from a representative of a well-established Hebrew organization. Several months before, I had choreographed a well-received dance to "Lilith" that I had performed in New York City and the surrounding areas. I was told that this organization wanted a video of my dance for their archives. Their mission was to compile everything available "about the demon Lilith"! Since my dance to Lilith was beautiful, I refused to give them a copy of my work. I was approached two more times and my answer was still "no." Immediately after the third attempt I developed a fervent desire to write this book because the truth should be told. *The First Sisters: Lilith and Eve* is a thought provoking work that challenges the age-old stigmas that have plagued women for a millennium. My analysis and re-interpretation is uniquely compelling. I hope to inspire my readers to question the foothold these unbalanced stories had on the human psyche. *The First Sisters: Lilith and Eve* defies yet defines the dichotomy between the Sacred Feminine and the male gods as it takes the reader on a journey of awareness.

I want to sincerely thank my husband Iain who gave his love, patient support and belief in the mission of this book. And to all the members of Sacred Moon Coven and the Witchcraft community in Salem, Massachusetts who have sent their Magick and much needed encouragement throughout this process.

Let *The First Sisters: Lilith and Eve* turn the patriarchal belief system upside.

Blessings,
Lady Haight-Ashton

Introduction

Was it just a word here or a word there in a very old biblical story that was changed or misinterpreted in translation altering the Feminine hierarchy's destiny?

The First Sisters: Lilith and Eve questions biblical myths from many directions.

It was said in the beginning, in a garden called Eden, that woman was created at the same time as man, and not from his rib. A first female created equal to stand as a first "partner" not a "wife." She was a person so troublesome that she vanishes from her rightful place in civilization's mythological legends in place of Eve, the first "wife." What if this story was meant to be told another way and it was this "female" as Lilith who was created first, before Adam?

With her younger sister Eve's story heralding the future of all womankind, Lilith and her story stands alone as a testament to the Sacred Feminine and man's fear of the mysteries that lie within her. I believe Lilith's story of "disobedience" marked a transition in our ancestors' thinking. Her defiance of Adam and subsequent banishment proclaimed a change that crept slowly into the world. It was a change so powerful that it threatened the very core of ancient beliefs. In many cultures positions of dominance switched as women were no longer valued on top or regarded as equal, but relegated to the bottom. With the additional legend of Eve's hereditary guilt to secure the transformation, the ancient matriarchal belief system was turned upside down.

Which inevitably brings us Lilith and Eve with their story as two sides of the same coin. Feminine empowerment and restraint. My purpose is not to re-tell an ancient story with a modern interpretation, but to invoke an "awakening." How potent is the power of suggestion through biblical words and how important those words were on the plight of womankind in the ancient Christian world and beyond ...

Lilith stands both as an icon to the downtrodden and an inspiration to the nonconformist that lurks in the minds of each of us. Her memory summons our fears as it sparks our motivation to experience life to the fullest without restraint or boundaries. She epitomizes freedom. Eve on the other hand shows us something different. Does she submit to temptation or not? History relives Eve's choice and the subsequent punishment of women through the ages. But how ironic that the cursed "apple" should ultimately become the staple of every happy normal family in the standard "apple pie"; but there are other thoughts on the Eve scenario. One is that it wasn't an apple at all but a pomegranate which is thought to be an aphrodisiac! And second, that the serpent was Lilith and she was simply reminding Eve of their sisterly connection. Their stories are different but they intertwine and together they define a compelling aspect of the Sacred Feminine.

If Lilith was allowed her rightful place, would her story and the plight of women have been non-existent? Thus, by stimulating these controversial and thought-provoking myths, I hope to take my readers on a journey of liberation.

One cannot begin to understand the ancient creation myths of Lilith and her sister Eve or their impact on civilizations' existence without first delving into the "real beginning" when societies of the pre-biblical Matriarchal era regarded females as the real-life symbols of the Great Goddess, the Primordial Mother of all.

As a necessary cover for the patriarchal authority to hide their fears, and as with her sister Eve, Lilith's story became one of the tools that would help control women's sexuality and thinking for thousands of years. Here was the dark unspoken cloud that must be hidden to be controlled. Lilith (Lili, Lilin. Lillake, Lilite. Lillet, Lamia) Temptress, Leader and Wise Woman, Goddess of the unknown you represent to your daughters the fundamental strength and determination of opportunity, freedom and sexual power and the attainment of knowledge. Sacred Divinity lives on in her image. Plus, her story further intrigues with the marriage of Lilith and Samael. From ancient texts beginning with Rabbi Isaac be Jacob ha-Kohen's "Treatise on the Left Emanation" and further references I share my research within the Kabbalah and other biblical texts including the Kabbalistic Demonology. I want my readers to understand the darkness that surrounds Lilith's image but to transcend it and embrace her amazing lightness.

The divorce of Lilith and Adam becomes final. As the ancient story unfolds, since Eve was formed out of Adam's rib, she was not his equal. Now there would be no doubt of her dependence, and the embarrassing question of feminine rights might never be raised again.

How can one fully comprehend the course that Lilith and Eve's story had on the female destiny as it traveled through the ages without also mentioning their sisters the Temple Priestess and her counterpart the Sacred Prostitute? As seers, sages, saints and sinners these women left their impact on history. In this chapter I discuss the earthly predecessors and successors to Lilith and Eve, the Priestess and her long reign that spanned every culture and era. Along with the Sacred Prostitute as her alter ego they influenced and enhanced the worship and beliefs of many different ancient societies. My intention is simply to create a thought provoking work. The story of the Temple Priestess and that of the Sacred Prostitute is just one thread in the story of Lilith and Eve's influence on society. As myths and stories traveled through the centuries their meanings altered as belief systems and political climates changed. And the pendulum swings back and forth on the myth or reality of these controversial women. They are the characters of dark tales whose images shake up our complacent realities.

Is their story myth or reality or both? Throughout history these women have been portrayed as sinners, saints and everything in between. They were also seers and sages. At times of great ritual and celebration these women channeled Divinity's ecstasy into their souls as the earthy representatives of the Goddess. I hope to acknowledge their prodigious value as wise women who aroused the Divine essence of the Sacred Feminine in their followers.

Lilith the original Serpent Goddess threads her way into many ancient mythologies. Inanna confronted her serpentine image in the deep recesses of Hades ... yet that moment helped catapult Inanna to her ultimate awakening and rebirth. And the thread of Lilith's imprint manifests in Crete and Delphi. This chapter opens an in-depth discussion of this spiraling tread and the Serpent Goddesses and their Priestesses who kept birthing Lilith's energy.

With the retelling of Lilith and Eve's myth, I invoke an awakening of the different sexual balance between female and male that could have been.

Lilith and Eve's message is passionate and rousing. I offer the readers charms, spells, meditations, invocations, rituals and prayers for men and women to channel Sacred Divinity in the guise of Lilith and Eve. Their message is passionate and rousing.

The world has been out of balance for a long time and so have we as humans. Male authoritarian religions have weighed down the Feminine. Let us come together and embrace both aspects within each of us, not as opposing but mirror images of each other. Perhaps as it was really meant to be. The ancient Yin to the Yang symbols of female and male are two circles within a never-ending spiral. It shows a symbol that is separate yet intertwined and balanced within. Acknowledging the Goddess as the Sacred Feminine and understanding the positive aspects of Lilith and Eve's story will help to right that balance. These two sisters with their "so-called" outspoken and rebellious acts should be viewed differently. Their actions should be regarded as a candid reminder to keep the Feminine hierarchy alive. We need to awaken.

When referencing Talmudic mythology, I found this

noteworthy quote:

> When studying the various teachings in the Talmud about demons, one immediately discovers references to the name Lilith. This is significant because today, the New Age movement speaks of "Lilith rising." Lilith is equated with a "first Eve," the feminine dark side of the divine and goddesses such as Isis, Astarte, the Black Madonna or Queen of Demons and other false gods. The myth of Lilith is a gnostic perversion of the Biblical account of Creation and Adam and Eve.[1]

The First Sisters: Lilith and Eve is a gateway to a provocative awakening.

Endnotes
1. http://watch.pairsite.com/HRtalmud.html

Chapter 1

In the Beginning – The Rise and Fall of the Sacred Feminine

From the first stirrings of human evolution our ancestors' memories became their stories, and our legends and myths. This vast cornucopia of ancient recollections and tales were recorded throughout time with body gestures, the first spoken sounds, in drawings and words etched into stone, written on parchment, painted on walls, vessels and animal skins, and carved upon monuments and tombs. Ancient records that awaken our quest again and again to unravel and understand the meaning of our existence, thus defined the principles and traditions of all civilizations for thousands of years. We have tales that vary immensely in their telling, but whose basis remains the same as each vainly attempts to answer the one overwhelming question, how did it all begin?

Thus, the abundance of creation myths became the foundation for varied stories that have run rampant in every culture and civilization. Each ancient tale usually follows a similar format whereby a Supreme Creator, either female or male, triggers a chain of events that results in the creation of the world. The well-known Hebrew-Christian myth that most of the so called "civilized" world ascribed to for millennia up to the present held on to a singular Supreme Being in the role of a male/father image. This male God took seven days to create our world and worked completely alone. Yet many other recorded beliefs recognized the importance of a Matriarchal figure and favored both a Mother and Father collaboration with the Mother usually doing most of the creating. The Aborigines of Australia's creation myth began when the Father of all Spirits awoke the Sun Mother who then created the lushness of the earth and later all of its creature inhabitants. It is said that she spoke to her birds and animals and fish and told them to live in peace while enjoying the fruits of the earth. Yet in other cultures such as the Japanese, creation began as an egg that burst forth as the earth with the Goddess Izanami later giving birth to the Sun and Moon. The influence of the feminine archetype as an egg is also prevalent in Greek mythology when the goddess of the night, Nyx, births Eros the god of love, from the primordial egg; the pieces of the shell becoming the Earth Goddess Gaia and the Sky God Uranus. Once again we have a collaboration of sorts with a very strong feminine element.

Once more the recurring theme plays out as the sky above is manifested and the earth below populated with creatures both animal and human, Grandmothers and Grandfathers to all peoples within a specific cultural format and timeframe.

And creation brought us the safety of the light and the fear of darkness. Let me quote from:

And God said, "Let there be light, and there was light." God saw that the light was good, and he separated the light from the darkness. God called the light "day," and the darkness he called "night." And there was evening, and there was morning – the first day.[1]

With light came all of creation. So why create darkness? Why deliberately create fear of an unknown? So, the underlying story of all creation myths eventually comes to the point when light meets dark thus opening up a metaphorical Paradise world.

How does this affect the strength of the Divine Feminine within ancient cultures? If creation myths brought safety along with fear, then they also brought rules, regulations inhibitions and instructions. What began in most cultures as a collaboration between Feminine and Masculine turned into inevitable power struggles. This imbalance brought a ruling strategy that not only added the creation of sin but conveniently supplied its inevitable consequences. Thus, from the very beginning of time the balance of equality was tipping.

Though science has marked humanity's evolution quite differently from the idea of "biblical creation," no matter what cultural, religious background or belief system you aspire to, the Old Testament biblical story of the creation of our mythological ancestors Adam and Eve is known to all. Ancient Judaic and later Christian rulers alike have used the moral of this ancient Hebrew story to regulate and discipline the cultural customs of humanity for millennia. Yet there was another more ancient legend that came before, one well known to a chosen few orthodox scholars and forbidden to others. Here we have a story with a far-reaching impact so controversial that its outcome was carefully yet quite brilliantly disguised as evil to conceal a real motivating fear. It was and still is the very basic fear of losing control. This is a story bound within the confines of ancient Jewish Mysticism, the story of Lilith, the first female of the ancient world and our first rebel. If Lilith's message had been allowed to flourish within a positive interpretation, her story would have changed the course of cultural inhibitions worldwide. Her influence would have elevated the role of women to unimaginable status. But as we know, it didn't happen that way.

Yet we have ancient Kabballah texts and biblical stories that have interested as well as disturbed scholars and orthodox believers for centuries and they read something like this: It was said in the beginning, in a garden called Eden, that female was created at the same time as man, and not from his rib. A first female created equal to stand as a first "partner" not a "wife." She was a person so troublesome that she vanishes from her rightful place in civilization's mythological legends in place of Eve, the first "wife." Scholars and theologians believe in their interpretation. But what if this creation story was meant to be told another way and it was this "female" as Lilith who was created first, before Adam?

With her younger Sister Eve's story heralding the future of all woman kind, Lilith and her story stands alone as a testament to the Sacred Feminine and man's fear of the mysteries that lie within her. I believe Lilith's story of "disobedience" marked a transition in our ancestors' thinking. It proclaimed a change that crept into the world, a change so powerful that it threatened the very core of ancient beliefs. In many cultures positions of dominance switched as women were no longer valued on top or regarded as equal,but relegated to the bottom. With the legend of Eve's hereditary guilt to secure the transformation, the ancient matriarchal belief system was turned upside down.

Yes, the Great Goddess as the Divine Feminine once reigned supreme only to be given the back door as new and more powerful and manipulative male dominated civilizations and religious fervor evolved. But was it just a word here or a word there in a very ancient story that was changed or misinterpreted in translation that helped alter the Feminine hierarchy's destiny?

One cannot begin to understand the ancient creation myths of Lilith and her sister Eve or their impact on civilization's existence without first delving into the "real beginning" when societies of the pre-biblical Matriarchal era regarded females as the real-life symbols of the Great Goddess, the Primordial Mother of all. Her many evolving images, a tribute to her influence upon the world's different societies, once dominated the ancient populations' thinking, understanding, environment and art. Though some cultures such as the Native American continued to revere a collaboration between Mother Earth and Father Sky, many other ancient cultures morphed their beliefs into a God as Father, thus simply deleting the influence of the Mother Goddess.

Past and modern archaeologists and historians have continuously disagreed upon the interpretation and importance of acknowledging ancient images of the feminine as Sacred

Divinity or earthbound female fertility totems. Though the historical misconception once swayed toward the latter, now more and more enlightened information and ideas are beginning to shift to a different reality. It is now the contemporary analysis, that perhaps these multi-media images ranging from the most primitive to the finest ornately stylized, were really ancestral images of the revered "Primordial Mother" the Goddess herself. It is this view of the Goddess that shows her importance to all of the ancient civilizations. And the Goddess is a woman. Thus, it proves that women's roles were once revered alongside the mysteries and the Magick of the universe. Women who brought life as the all-giving and all-nurturing vessels also reminded their male partners of their worth and their role in the scheme of existence. Here lies the universal complexity of humanity. Not only did the mystery of life grow and come from within a woman's body, but our ancient male ancestors' chief weakness lay in their inability to understand the miracle. It bred fear of the unknown, as in the void darkness of the night. And yet the feminine also held the power of desire in man's inability to resist every woman's power of allure. Nonetheless it is still a freethinking and open-minded person with the strength to comprehend and embrace our true ancestral mythologies who can now join others in unraveling the compelling significance of the mystery of "Herstory" as it was meant to be.

Yet sadly (as seen on many cable television documentaries) newly discovered archeological sites are still unearthing ancient objects that in too many instances are even now being labeled as "fertility objects." Are we still misrepresenting our common human roots by undermining the true value of these symbols of the Sacred Feminine, the Goddess, in the evolution of so many ancient societies?

Beyond drawings, statutes and myths, what of the ancient temple ruins that still exist as broken effigies to once thriving Goddess cultures? These were vibrant mysterious structures where sacred Priestesses dwelt as earthly representatives of the Divine Feminine. Here they lived, worshipped, danced and used their clairvoyant skills to foretell the future and most of all honor a Matron Goddess. Delphi famously known as a temple to the God Apollo originally housed such a matron Goddess. According to Homeric hymns it was the Great Mother Gaia who originally founded the Delphic Oracle Temple/Shrine at Delphi in Greece and inspired its original python or serpent High Priestess called the Pythia. In all cultures, the ageless serpent, so intimately bound to the earth, was originally identified with the Great Mother Goddess Herself. The Greeks called the Great Mother Gaia or Gaea (Ge=earth). From her, heaven (Uranies) and sea (Pontos) were born and she became the Mother of all, a cornucopia filled with the fruits of the earth.

Thus, the earthbound serpent, once revered as a symbol of the Goddess, morphs into association with both of our naughty sisters Lilith and Eve. Yet the altered serpent's imprint continues to snake through history's timeline again and again in story after story as one of the most ancient and hidden reminders of the female mysteries. Women and serpents both represent the Magickal power of life. Ancient matriarchal societies viewed the serpent as a sign of immortality because of their mysterious living ritual of shedding their skin, thus seeming to be renewed again and again. Serpents thus held the mysterious secret of life with this repetition of their shedding ritual. To our ancient patriarchal fathers, women also shared this mystery and wonder as their bodies held the ability to bring forth new life again and again. So over two millennia ago matriarchal power held court at the great Temple shrines of Delphi where the ancient Greeks thought of the Mother Goddess Gaia as mother of the Divine Female Serpent. The name "Delphi" comes from "Delphyne" which means the great snake of the Mother, the ancient word "delphys" means womb. The serpent was thought to come from the bowels of the earth, the Great Mother's womb. The sacred python was housed in the Doric Temple at Delphi in the omphalos, or "navel shrine," the center of the earth. The shrine was built underground in a beehive shape. Questions were asked of the Pythia or High Priestess who originally channeled the spirit of the Great Goddess and later as more accepted "historical" interpretation relates, the God Apollo. During her prophecies, the Pythia Priestess as "Oracle" of the ancient Hellenic World would rest her hand on the omphalos as the spoken prophecy came from her lips. She passed her judgment on the past, present, and future acts of the Greeks. The long winding road called "The Sacred Way" from Athens to Delphi, still snakes over black cliffs and along the high, narrow mountain paths. The ancient ruins of Delphi can be seen as broken columns blazing white in the sun. The Oracle's dark prophetic cave-shrine is seen as a perfect balance between the sky above and the sea below. If the ruins could talk what would they say the Oracle predicted?

Interesting though somewhat disturbing was a recent program that I watched on a popular cable channel. It was about Delphi and the sacred Oracle. Here we had the great Prophetesses of the ancient world depicted as downgraded Priestesses who retained very little to no psychic powers, and who spoke in confusing riddles and abstract generalities so that their words could be either right or wrong depending upon the interpretation. I was appalled though not surprised to see that the ancient fears and prejudices were still very much alive today.

The Goddess Inanna the Sumerian Queen of Heaven and Earth, appearing as early as ca. 4000 to 3100 BCE, (her image oftentimes confused with that of Lilith) confronts her own feminine mysteries through the symbolic serpent in her underworld descent into the Netherland. The story of Inanna's descent was originally discovered as a poem carved upon an ancient and broken stone tablet. Here the snake/serpent, thought to be a bold reminder of Lilith, symbolizes Inanna's innermost fears of her own sexuality which she faces in her darkest and deepest underground moment. (To acknowledge Lilith in her many guises one learns to overcome trepidation and openly embrace the power and mysteries of the Sacred Feminine.) From this experience into the Earth's depths Inanna then ascends up into the sky's light to be reborn and transformed into her Divinity. But it is here that the story changes meaning. The male hero Gilgamesh, so the tale relates, drives the serpent away thus awakening Inanna's passion and allowing her to claim her throne and "bed."

To acknowledge Lilith's influence on Inanna's experience is to accept that it was not only a journey through life's phases but the depths of darkness as well. Inanna confronted her symbolic death (the death of the Sacred Feminine) to be reborn into a different and not as welcoming era.

As we move back and forth within the historical timeline in our evolution of pre and post Lilith and Eve, we come to the dawn of Christianity, the time of Mary the Madonna and Mary Magdalene the whore. History now gives us a new, yet familiar concept, of the good girl, bad girl scenario, one that already played out in the ancient legends of our "Sisters" Lilith and Eve. One Mary, with her hair bound under a veil, was supposedly so pure that her womb became fertile without physical contact, a sort of spontaneous combustion. Her polar opposite appears as Mary Magdalene, an impure "whore," outspoken, intelligent and beautifully alluring with long flowing snake-like tresses. Here are two opposite ends of the spectrum in the ancient world of repressed Divine Femininity. Yet both were named Mary and though somewhat differently, both loved the same man! Has "Herstory" also lost something here in translation and were these female images meant to portray aspects of the same persona!

Again, we have the sensual serpent so often identified as a potent symbol of the Great Mother herself (morphing into Lilith) oftentimes depicted in old Christian statutes as lying beneath and around the naked feet of Mary the Madonna as she stands upon the world or encircling the crescent moon that Mary's feet balance upon. Is this symbolic imagery a slap to the pre-Christian era? Perhaps so, yet there might also be another possible analysis. Is the serpent wrapped around the world below the Madonna's feet an ancient reminder that the influence of the Great Mother Goddess' reign as the Sacred Divinity, in the guise of Lilith, never really left the world? Is the crescent moon displayed as the "Heavenly Crown" or "horns" of Isis, and placed under the Madonna's feet an ancient remembrance of the enduring power the Goddess of 10,000 names had before the new Christian religions heralded the eventual suppression of all that came before?

As a small child brought up as a strict Catholic, I looked upon these statutes in awe and often wondered about the unique symbolism they so carefully displayed.

From Goddess to Saint and back again, the ages tell of Divinity once lost but never forgotten. Thus the sacred, revered image of the Great Isis, the ancient Egyptian Goddess of 10,000 names, evolved into the Catholics' most venerated Saint, the Madonna, Blessed Mary the Mother of Jesus. There are as many ancient statues and depictions of Isis cradling her son Horus on her lap as modern renderings of Mary with her son Jesus. How better to welcome new and perhaps skeptical converts to the carefully orchestrated changes that lay ahead.

Going beyond the Isis and Madonna similarity, it is also well known in New Age and pagan circles that in order for the ancient religions to accept Christianity along with newly written biblical conventions, it was necessary to disguise and change the most familiar and honored Goddess symbols into Saintly ones.

Another example is the Goddess Brighid, Mother of the Celts also known as Brid, Bridget or Brede who had such a sustaining presence among her people that when Christianity came to Ireland she was the only Goddess who became a Saint. As a Goddess her Feminine Divinity was not only a solitary presence but also her triple Goddess form as a poet, metalsmith and healer.

> The Christian Saint Bridget was known as "Bridget, daughter of Dubhteach, of KillDara." The nineteen virgins who tended the sacred flame of Killdara became nineteen holy nuns who served the Saint, who was said to have been ordained so she could celebrate Mass like a priest.[2]

I recently read an interesting book titled *Confessions of a Pagan Nun* by Kate Horsley. This fictional account recounted in diary entries the memories of a female Druid Priestess's journey of understanding and survival as a Nun in the monastery of Saint Brigit. It re-counts the time of upheaval, turmoil and ultimate acquiescence of the Celtic peoples as the Christian transition takes its strangling hold. Though fictional in content, Kate Horsley nonetheless describes a format that probably did exist, for Priestesses to transition to Nuns and thus for Goddesses to transition to Saints. How apropos that the monastery's patron saint in the book was St. Brigit.

Not all feminine Saints started out as Goddesses. Let us return again to the well-known representation of St. Mary Magdalene with her snake-like coiling "Lilith" tresses. Long and flowing hair wrapped around and caressing her female form, was the same abundant hair that dried Jesus' feet. An important date in the story of Mary Magdalene is 325 CE when the Council of Nicaea took place by order of the Roman Emperor Caesar Flavius Constantine. As her own hidden Gospel banned to all at the Council of Nicaea relates, she was intelligent, strong and "the most trusted." It was here that the Emperor Constantine presided over a group of Church bishops and leaders. Christian history records that his goal was to define the one true Jesus Christ as the one true Christian God for all of Christianity. Questions had persisted as to how to identify Christ? Was he more divine than human or more human than divine? The Council of Nicaea affirmed the male Apostles' teachings of who Christ was, need I say more? Yet Mary Magdalene held onto her important role not only as a disciple, but perhaps even more until "Herstory" was changed to history. Thus her once good and "trusted" image became distorted with each written gospel and instead of becoming a revered image for womankind she was portrayed as a redeemed bad girl, who was only given Sainthood as a gift for her deep repentance! In each mythological story about a powerful feminine character the ending seems to follow a predictable pattern of her rise and fall when "Herstory" changes to history. Another well-known example of the rise and fall scenario is the story of St. Joan of Arc, so reminiscent of the Goddess Athena, in her warrior woman persona.

> When Joan was about 12 years old, she began hearing "voices" of St. Michael, St. Catherine, and St. Margaret believing them to have been sent by God. These voices told her that it was her divine mission to free her country from the English and help the dauphin gain the French throne. They told her to cut her hair, dress in man's uniform and pick-up the arms.[3]

Later as history reports, the inquisition re-interpreted the voices she heard as those of the devil and found evil in the way she dressed. She was then tried, convicted and later burned at the stake as a heretic. Once again, we have the life of a woman who had a tremendous impact on society and whose supposed fall from grace is total until after her death when forgiveness was once again rewarded with Saintly status by the Christian patriarchs.

But not all infamous female figures morphed into Christian saints. Beyond Lilith and Eve who remained icons of disobedience and projected images not interpreted as saintly, we have a striking example in the tale of the divinely powerful Queen Boadicea.

It is said that between 61 CE and 63 CE she miraculously led her people, the Iceni Celts, to victory against the Romans. Sadly, her victory was short lived and she ultimately suffered defeat, capture and humiliation. Though not in the forefront of modern heroes or considered an ancient Goddess, she does remain for many one of the greatest heroines of Britain and a tribute to the Divine Feminine.

Finally, one cannot understand the far reaching impact of Lilith's serpent threads in history without mentioning the tale of St. Patrick who drove the serpents from Ireland when none had ever existed there! Surely that was simply a metaphor for removal of the old Goddess religion and its followers as portrayed by the mysterious serpent whose place in the dark annals of pre-Christian civilization held fast to its connection to the Divine Feminine. Did he try to drive the power and influence of Lilith's serpent persona from our consciousness?

Divinity as the Sacred Feminine is also about beauty and love. The sensually famous Goddesses of Love, Venus and Aphrodite so often depicted in numerous forms of stylized art for centuries, were well aware of their feminine powers of allure and used them to good advantage. We tend to lose our edge as women when we deny or try to mask our intrinsic alluring and ultimate Goddess-given feminine power. Is it natural for women to deny their genetic strengths, the very strengths that make us superbly different? Perhaps Lilith was the first, yet there are other stories and myths that abound of women who made a lasting impact on culture by embracing and effectively using their Divine Feminine fatale aspects. Everyone knows the story of Cleopatra who in my opinion was totally in touch with her Goddess Diana persona with a little Aphrodite allure thrown in for good measure. And the character of Shakespeare's Juliet totally channeled the innocence of the Goddess Persephone alongside the determination of the Norse Goddess Freya. I like to think of their rise as empowering and their fall as the unfortunate outcome of a male-dominated society with too many clouded misinterpretations.

Our ancient Goddess-worshipping ancestors both female and male, understood and also saw the sacred mysteries of life and death in the phases of the New, Full, and Waning/Dark Moons which symbolically correspond to the phases of a woman's life. The ever present Divine Feminine also gave civilizations the basic theme of these three phases in the form of the Triple Goddess who can be found in the different mythologies of all peoples and whose theory remains alive to this day. She is the Maiden, Mother and Crone. She represents the enchanting innocence of youth, the full ripeness of motherhood and the enlightened wisdom of age in every woman's life. The view of the Goddess as a triple aspect goes back as far as recorded history (perhaps further). The concept is embodied in many myths, and legends, and throughout many cultures. The Three Fates, The Muses, Norns, Moire, Gorgons, The Three Graces, The Charities are just a few of the trinity personas. The energy of the Triple Goddess is still alive in the universe and actively inside each woman. It is transforming energy, just as the seasons transform, so we transform and change from Maidens, to Mothers, to Crones, then back again to Maidens. In the spiraling "wheel of the year," for the ancient Celts and now also witches and pagans who honor the Goddess, the wise Crone of autumn's Samhain becomes the youthful Maiden of the spring equinox.

Despite the many media images of the ultimate "woman" each and every one of us is beautiful no matter what our shape or our age. Since societies all over the world frown upon the "female" aging process, women of every century have tried in vain to keep their youthful magnetism alive. If we could only ignore the hype of an unbalanced patriarchal world and accept that age brings its rewards. Age and the wealth of experiences that accompanies it can bestow wisdom and understanding upon any individual who welcomes the physical change whether female or male. But to women who have dealt with millennia of age stigmas, rethinking does not come easily. As a woman who has tasted the joys of spring and summer and now looks towards life's autumn, I look upon any and all women of age as simply women of splendor. The outward body is merely a shell to house the inner soul which is a true glimpse of the real person. Though the body might experience changes, each little shift of time announces to the world a woman's accomplishments and strengths. Age is wisdom. Now if society would only catch on to this thought! The Sacred Feminine knows no boundaries.

As set forth by common history this transforming triple aspect was re-interpreted as a celestial trinity for patriarchal Catholics and other Christians by becoming "the father, son and holy spirit." Thus, re-defining Feminine Divinity once again and dissolving it into a manageable masculine persona. The most compelling Christian story of the trinity or triple aspect and one that is not often welcomed is that of the "Three Marys" who together washed Jesus' body in preparation for burial. They were St. Mary Magdalene, Blessed Mary the Madonna, and St. Mary Salome, Mother of St. James. It is interesting that the third Mary was also named Salome. Biblical references to "another" Salome's adventures are anything but flattering and she is anything but saint like, though she was ever so powerful and wise in her "Lilith" fascination. So, does this trinity of "Marys" clandestinely encompass a threading connection to the Feminine Divinity as Mary Magdalene the Maiden, Mary the Madonna as Mother and Mary Salome the Crone?

> Behold the Three-Formed Goddess;
> She who is ever Three – Maid, Mother, and Crone.
> Yet she is ever One;
> She in all women, and they all in her.
> Look at these Three who are one, with fearless love,
> That you too may be whole.[4]

Throughout time man has feared what he did not understand. And common thought prescribes that what is feared most must be controlled or how could one survive?

Endnotes

1. Genesis 1
2. www.technoharp.com/Brighidsplace
3. Quoted from the Catholic online female Saints pg. http://www.catholic.org/saints/
4. Excerpted from the Witches' Goddess Volume II, Janet and Stewart Farrar pg. 75

Chapter 2

Lilith: Birth of the Equal

Many years ago, I was immersed in a personal journey of Goddess discovery and research. I reveled in the mythologies and legends of the Great Goddess Isis whose sacred temple worship exists even now (see www.fellowshipofisis.com); Hecate the Magickal and powerful crone Mother; Bridget, Goddess of the Celts and Selket whose ancient image was discovered guarding Tutankhamen's tomb thus thrusting her beautiful and enigmatic persona into our consciousness. I found so many incredible and compelling stories of Goddesses with their earthy and mystical strengths, yet there was something missing. Something within my soul drew me deeper and deeper into this research. I was on a quest for understanding and enlightenment that could only be satisfied with immersion into the first ancient myths carved in stone and painted upon parchment, the significant shifting legends that heralded the moment of transition when the "Great Primordial Goddess" once so firmly planted in consciousness, slipped from our grasp.

Perhaps for me it was finding the answer buried within ancient Jewish mysticism in the Kabbalah whose origins perhaps date as early as the first century CE[1] in Sumerian and Babylonian legends, stories and art; and Old Testament references to name a few.

Lilith (Hebrew לילית) is a mythological female Mesopotamian storm demon associated with wind and was thought to be a bearer of disease, illness, and death. The figure of Lilith first appeared in a class of wind and storm demons or spirits as Lilitu, in Sumer, circa 4000 BC. Many scholars place the origin of the phonetic name "Lilith" at somewhere around 700

BC despite post-dating even the time of Moses. Lilith appears as a night demon in Jewish lore and as a screech owl in the King James version of the Bible.

Hebrew לילית Lilit, Akkadian Līlītu are female nisba adjectives from the Proto-Semitic root LYL "night", literally translating to nocturnal "female night being/demon", although cuneiform inscriptions where Līlīt and Līlītu refers to disease-bearing wind spirits exist.

Another possibility is association not with "night" but with "wind"; i.e. identification of Akkadian Lil-itu as a loan from Sumerian lil, "air" — specifically from NIN.LIL "lady air", goddess of the South wind and wife of Enlil — and itud, "moon".

The Akkadian masculine līlû shows no nisba suffix and has been compared to Sumerian (kiskil-) lilla.[2]

Within these words of identity as a storm Goddess, seductive demon and nighttime spirit, I sought and hopefully found the true hidden story/legend of Lilith. Notoriously known as the fabled succubus of Kabbalah and biblical renown, she was the timeless femme fatale, who tempted the weaker sex. She is acclaimed as the Goddess of wet dreams who preyed on her male victims as they slept.

Just the magnetism of her name bequeathed dread in the souls of the unwary. But in her ancient beginning she was simply the first partner whom God created as equal to her mate Adam. Together they would live in the lush splendor of a paradise called the Garden of Eden as unfettered partners. How momentarily naïve and yet when one adds ego, how tempting is wisdom and then power. The equal female to the male who chose to leave the Garden Paradise rather than sexually lie beneath and become subordinate to the husband she was given by the male God.

Now there is a resurgence of curiosity and an immense growing awareness of her compelling and very ancient story, but many years ago when my interest first blossomed, it was not so. During my Lilith "awakening" I found it exciting to unearth every word of her myth and even more exciting to discover the impact her ancient secrets held in re-defining the Feminine role that spiraled downward through the ages. And sadly what I discovered was an extensive carefully crafted deception of the most damaging and negative press imaginable. Yet I fell deeply into the ancient and positive aura of the primordial Lilith. Was she once revered as a Goddess? Perhaps we will never know. By reading between the historical lines of biblical text, I found that she really represented the first woman of equality and with that status was and is a true Goddess persona. In each written and spoken word of her story one discovers that she was a woman of substance, well before her time. For me and many other awakened women she was and still is a true Goddess of the Sacred Feminine with unbridled strength and confidence in her sexual powers.

Many years ago, in my impassioned quest for all things Lilith I was given a copy of a Liturgy/poem. At the time I was told the author was anonymous. Much later I found a reference in this website: (http://www.lilithinstitute.com/creations/creations. htm) now being attributed to the writer Cosi Fabian in1991. This Liturgy has become an overwhelming inspiration as well as my daily mantra.

Liturgy for Lilith

I am Lilith, Grandmother of Mary Magdalene.

I am Lilith, whose sexual fire was too hot for God.

I am Lilith, the First Woman, who chose the rage of exile over the cancer

Of servitude.

I am Lilith, Mother to the Mother-less.

I am Lilith, whose blood covers the moon.

I am Lilith, standing on owls' claws at a woman's crossroads.

I am Lilith, the Whore in the gateway of the Temple.

I am Lilith, whose serpentine tongue caused Eve to laugh, and pick the apple!

I am Lilith, Revolving Sword of Flame – scorching hypocrisy from truth's white bones.

I am Lilith, free-moving in the Wilderness.

I am Lilith, spirit of night and air.

I am Lilith, in whose dark caves transgressors find sanctuary.

I am Salome.

I am Morgan le Faye.

I am the Queen of Shayba –

My hair is black, and I am "dark but comely,"

(Solomon sang my song!).

My hair is red and my skin, ivory.

I am Eve's big sister.

I am Lilith, Mother to the motherless.

I am Lilith, whose sexual fire was too hot for God.

I am Lilith, living in the Shadow.

Waiting. For you.

Lilith's story as an outspoken ground breaker whose determination to be acknowledged as the viable equal seems surprisingly natural. Oddly equality has been the age-old issue that seems to plague humanity even now. Yet, it seems her story was created simply so that a questionable lesson of importance could be learned by her (and all feminine sovereignty), being thrown into the depths of forbidden obscurity. As a necessary cover for the patriarchal authority to hide their fears, and as with her sister Eve, Lilith's story became one of the tools that would help control women's sexuality and independent thinking for thousands of years. Here was the dark unspoken cloud that must be hidden to be controlled. Was this the first ancient reminder for men to never allow their wives and daughters to transgress from their staunch patriarchal rule or see them condemned to unthinkable punishment, as ancient texts recall? Lilith's downfall from grace was thrust on her by those in authority, not Lilith, who saw her own decision as simply standing up for herself and her rights as an equal. It was said in text after text that she was created by the male God as an equal partner to Adam. As was her equal right, she chose not to lie beneath Adam and assume an inferior sexual position. For that act she was duly punished. I ask men and women alike, was her decision so very bad? Imagine a world where this story was told in a positive light as the story of a strong resilient woman whose sexuality was equal if not above that of her male partner, literally! Yet we still live in a hypocritical world in an environment that has never truly understood or embraced equality in its pure unbiassed sense.

Perhaps if history gave us an accepted acknowledgement of equality we women wouldn't have had such a long arduous journey to fight back authority and reclaim our feminine rights. Battles won to gain the right to vote, the right to hold property and the right to make our own decisions … out of bound feet and bondage and into the light! Let us imagine a matriarchal society where women are not only revered within their rightful places as maidens, mothers and crones, but understood as thinkers, leaders and vessels of the Sacred Divine. Sadly, history has shown that we have sometimes been our own worst enemies. But dismissing that thought for a more positive outlook, we must learn to truly accept ourselves. Throughout "Herstory" women such as Lilith have spoken out and fought hard to be regarded as equal to men. Lilith was the first brave woman with a mind of her own and that is to be applauded.

I oftentimes find myself explaining and defending Lilith's openly sexual and irreverent story to my female and male friends. I am always dumbfounded with the realization that so many of us do not see our tendencies to conform, to walk a safe pathway and that as women we might have been programmed to think within those boundaries. I now speak to those brave women who see clearly, are empowered, bold and ethnically diverse, and who see themselves as confident in their individual strengths. It is our subliminal Lilith strength that speaks to us in our shared common thread as mothers, artists, dancers, politicians, businesswomen and homemakers and on and on. Whether we want to admit it or not the reality is that "history" has brainwashed women for thousands of years to contain and re-direct their aspirations for fear of reprisal. Since the ancient transition from matriarchal to patriarchal, in most societies women have been brought up to deny their inner feminine powers and their right to choose as completely frivolous, inadequate and unintelligent. With actions, words and persecution the message of a Divine Feminine through the Goddess was thought to be successfully suppressed, yet it has survived within each of us individually and culturally. No matter the color, race or cultural background, women are all sisters under the skin. With each telling of Lilith's spellbinding story as it was really meant to be relayed, I can see the spark of light and recognition in all of my sisters' eyes.

What really happened to the once powerful reign of the Divine Feminine? How began the multi-leveled female descent into subservience and misconceptions?

Here is the most ancient and controversial mythology, I give you my research and my personal understanding of the legend of the fabled yet nefarious Lilith.

Let us start at the beginning of one of the most hidden and least known of the ancient "creation" mythological stories, biblical or otherwise. In the most ancient and earliest verbal and written Hebrew traditions, the symbol/persona of the first Primordial/Earth Mother, originally began as Lilith, the first "Equal Partner" not Eve, the first subservient "wife." So before we can acknowledge the impact and many varied views on the story of the more common feminine archetype of Eve it is important to acknowledge the birth, life and unfair demise into the depths of darkness of the very first female who embodied all of the mysteries and complexities of Sacred Feminine Divinity, Lilith.

Lilith has her birth related in ancient patriarchal Hebrew legends within Talmudic and Kabbalistic writings incorporating many intriguing deviations. In the *Hebrew Goddess*, Raphael Patai mentions a number of variations.

According to one, she was created before Adam, in fact on the fifth day of Creation, because the "living creature" with whose swarms God filled the waters[3] [...] was none other than Lilith.[4] [...] Another version, which ties in directly with the earlier Talmudic Lilith image, recounts that she was created by God in the same manner in which He has shortly before fashioned Adam. [...] That is to say, God again turned to the earth to obtain raw material, but this time, instead of using clean earth which was the substance of Adam's body, He— for reasons unknown—took filth and impure sediments from the earth, and out of these He formed a female. As was to be expected this creature turned out to be evil.[5] [...] According to a third version, God originally created Adam and Lilith together in such a manner that the female creature was contained in the male ...[6]

[...] Yet another version considers Lilith not as a being created by God, but as a divine entity which emerged spontaneously, either out of the Great Supernal Abyss, or out of the power-aspect of God ...[7]

Quoting from *The Alphabet of Ben Sira* (Genesis 2:28):

After God created Adam, who was alone, He said, "It is not good for man to be alone."

He then created a woman for Adam, from the earth, as He had created Adam himself, and called her Lilith. Adam and Lilith immediately began to fight. She said, "I will not lie below," and he said, "I will not lie beneath you, but only on top. For you are fit only to be in the bottom position, while I am to be the superior one." Lilith responded, "We are equal to each other inasmuch as we were both created from the earth." But they would not listen to one another. When Lilith saw this, she pronounced the Ineffable Name and flew away into the air. Adam stood in prayer before his Creator: "Sovereign of the universe!" he said, "the woman you gave me has run away." At once, the Holy One, blessed be He, sent these three angels to bring her back [...] Said the Holy One to Adam, "If she agrees to come back, fine. If not, she must permit one hundred of her children to die every day." The angels left God and pursued Lilith, whom they overtook in the midst of the sea, in the mighty waters wherein the Egyptians were destined to drown. They told her God's word, but she did not wish to return. The angels said, "We shall drown you in the sea." "Leave me!" she said ...[8]

Lilith had to become God's Hebrew Goddess consort in order to learn and use the unspoken name to escape Adam (p. 240H). Lilith used whatever power was at her disposal to save herself from physical and mental domination.

While thus Zohar and the later Kabbalists who were influenced by it attribute God's degradation through coupling with Lilith to the cosmic consequences of the destruction of the Temple, the pre-Zoharic Gnostic Kabbalists such as Moses of Burgos, place the same divine Fall in the very days of Creation.[9]

The struggle continues until Lilith becomes so frustrated with Adam's stubbornness and arrogance that she brazenly pronounces the Tetragrammaton, the ineffable name of the Lord. God's name (YHWH), translated as "Lord God" in most Bibles and roughly equivalent to the term "Yahweh," has long been considered so holy that it is unspeakable. During the days of the Jerusalem Temple, only the High Priest said the word out loud, and then only once a year, on the Day of Atonement. In Jewish theology and practice, there is still mystery and majesty attached to God's special name. The Tetragrammaton is considered "the name that comprises all."[10]

In the Bible's burning bush episode of Exodus 3, God explains the meaning of the divine name as "I am what I am," or "I will be what I will be," a kind of formula for YHWH (vuvh), associated with the Hebrew root "to be." The whole of the Torah is thought to be contained within the holy name. In The Alphabet, Lilith sins by impudently uttering the sacred syllables, hereby demonstrating to a medieval audience her unworthiness to reside in Paradise. So, Lilith flies away, having gained power to do so by pronouncing God's avowed name. Though made of the earth, she is not earthbound. Her dramatic departure reestablishes for a new generation Lilith's supernatural character as a winged devil.[11]

With such personal familiarity to the so-called "creator," could she have been the original Goddess to the God? Could Lilith have really represented one of the original and perhaps most powerful ancient Mother Goddess personas, once so revered in our earliest civilizations? But if so this Divine story was completely downgraded and interpreted through the ages to become a demon's mythology?

Lilith and her story was actually the first harsh written lesson for womankind. "Herstory" appears in text after ancient text describing the consequences faced by women if they stood up for themselves and acted accordingly. The ancient moral for women seemed to evolve within the confines of conformity, submission and obedience!

As the myths surrounding Lilith continue to be recorded we can see a pattern form whereby the patriarch's rationale became the accepted cultural view. How better to explain Lilith's so called bad behavior in standing up to Adam than to change her "equal" birth into one that became tainted and muddied. If Lilith was created bad at birth then her behavior was more easily explained. The onus is off both God and Adam for making any judgmental mistakes. Male purity and superiority was then assured and thus patriarchal dogma not only survived but continues with falsehoods and control over women in many cultures even now. With Lilith's story twisted to explain her behavior away as simply "bad from birth" and with the burden of Eve's innocent bite, what chance did women have in such an authoritarian world.

The Rosicruciana and Fellow of American Academy of Astrologians, Grace Ellery Williams has written:

> The difference between the two creations of man and woman critically examined was recognized by the rabbins, and their speculations on the subject laid the basis for the further legend that the woman created at the same time with Adam, and therefore not the woman formed from his rib, was the first wife, and turned out badly.[12]

Lilith had obtained her wings of freedom and flight. She flew out of the first Garden of Eden but not necessarily out of sight. Lilith's story was once studied and interpreted within ancient manuscripts by those few aged scholars who had the understanding and strength to resist her overpowering allure. She was hidden away from the uneducated who did not have the mental tools to comprehend her power beyond their protective amulets and magickal cures. Now a revival interest in Lilith can be found throughout the internet on numerous reference sites and web pages, in various printed books and articles, and within newly unearthed and available quotes from ancient texts.

Here are a few examples of these no longer obscure ancient passages. Are these truly unflattering references to Lilith and is she possibly referred to as the screech owl? In the Book of Revelations there is a passage from the prophet Isaiah 34:14 that reads: "The wild beasts of the desert shall also meet with the wild beasts of the island, and the satyr shall cry to his fellow; the screech owl also shall be there, and find for herself a place to rest."[13] Regarding the "heavenly war" Revelations, 12:14 describes: "But the woman was given two great eagle's wings, to fly to the place in the wilds where for three years and a half she was to be sustained, out of reach of the serpent."[14] (What an obvious analogy!)

Runaway Lilith found by the angels at the Red Sea remained inflexible, openly accepting her fate, and rather unique doomful fiendish status. Since she refused to yield and return to Adam to be a slave to his needs, she morphs into the original female demon and her story becomes the blueprint for the creation of the Succubus myth. With the fear of Lilith and her power of fascination so strong the ancient texts brought her forth as the original Succubus.

A Succubus is defined as "a demon in female form, said to have sexual intercourse with men in their sleep. Any demon or evil spirit. A strumpet or prostitute."[15]

Beyond her succubus image of midnight romps with dreaming men, Lilith was also believed to steal their semen and thus become pregnant from them and bear thousands of demonic children every night who would die in infancy.

Another convoluted myth emerged with Lilith having the power of life and death over all children after birth until their eighth day of existence. Is this why Christian churches at one time baptized infants before the eighth day of life? And blessed them in the names of the new patriarchal trinity, the Father and the Son and the Holy Ghost (later Spirit), words that Christians believed had the potency to drive away evil. To this day some strict religious Hebrew sects still place amulets near a newborn's crib to ward off Lilith from coming and sucking away the infant's soul.

I find ancient charms and amulets fascinating with their need to protect against fears of the unknown. My research unearthed this interesting one relating to the infamous Lilith whose far reaching fame stretched all the way to Italy where *Stregheria* is known as Italian Witchcraft. Here is a unique and ancient reference to Lilith as a "Witch."

Here is a charm against Lilith as a "Striga," a witch, dated 1531 CE.

Black Striga, black and black
Blood shall eat and blood shall drink;
Like an ox she shall bellow
Like a bear she shall growl
Like a wolf she shall crush.[16]

The Succubus is also said to mate and then destroy her lovers. Here we have a simple description in nature of the Queen Bee whose worker bees and hives give us the sweet temptation of honey. How many other earthly creatures adhere to this system?

Yet it is worth noting that the Succubus had a counterpart in the Incubus. Not to be undone, our ancient patriarchs gave us the "incubus" (Latin, "to lie upon") who haunted women. These demon lovers were thought to assume human form to visit their victims in the dead of night, sometimes taking on the appearance of the unknowing victim's spouse or lover. The incubus had the ability to paralyze the victim, or even to cause all of the occupants of a house to fall into a stupor while it carried out its evil deeds. Sex with an incubus was described as an unpleasant, often painful affair.

"The origins of the sexual demon go back to the beginnings of civilization – the Assyrian legend of Lilith the Night Hag whose children became the lili, who roamed about at night satisfying their endless lust with human men."[17]

Instead of tainting her earthly sisters with her so-called "succubus personality" our downgraded maiden Lilith was until recently suppressed from most common biblical mythology. Eve on the other hand stayed alive to mate and become the handmaiden of the "original sin." This brings us to an interesting and important conceptual and haunting conclusion within Lilith's story. Her ouster from "paradise," though a grievous disobedience wasn't referred to as a "sin" in the Christian world, as was her sister Eve's temptation!

As the saga of Lilith continues there are many references to her "demon" offspring. Sadly these stories are abundant, this one in particular seems to be less noxious.

According to legend, before Eve, God made Lilith, much as He made Adam. Although Adam considered himself the superior, Lilith didn't agree, claiming she was her own person. They quarreled constantly (particularly about sex, some sources state), until finally Lilith became enraged and fled the Garden of Eden. She settled in a cave, where her relations with demons produced the first of her children. Unlike the "original" demons, Lilith and her hybrid children are typically malicious and actively seek to harm humans in one way or another.[18]

Lilith's image was once thoroughly hidden and even the sound of her name was pronounced with extreme caution. She was systematically and deliberately stripped of her Mother Goddess image. How strong is the influence of a conjured-up story, based on the unrealistic fear of the deeply sexual and mysterious Divine Feminine?

"In medieval times, the Christian church called her Mother of the Witches, and projected on to women all these feared so-called attributes of Lilith. Christians united with Jews and Moslems in their fear of her."[19]

Grace Ellery Williams, Fellow, American Academy of Astrologians states:

It was natural to assign the name of this wife, to one of the ancient goddesses who had been degraded into demonesses. For the history of Mariolatry in northern Europe has been many times anticipated; the mother's tenderness and devotion, the first smile of love upon social chaos, availed to give every race its Madonna, whose popularity drew around her the fatal favors of the priestcraft, weighing her down at last to be a type of corruption. Even the Semitic tribes with their hard masculine deities, seemed to have once worshiped Alilat, whose name survives as Elohim and Allah. Among those degraded Madonnas was Lilith, whose name has been found in a Chaldean inscription, which says, "when a country is at peace, 'Lilith' (Lilatu) is not before them." The name is from Assyrian lay'la, Hebrew Lil (night) which already in Accadian meant sorcery. It probably personified the darkness that soothed children to slumber; and the word Lullaby has been derived from Lilith Abi. The theory may suggest the path by which the soft southern night came to mean a nocturnal specter.[20]

The mysteries of Lilith in ancient Hebrew texts never cease to confound the reader. These intricate myths take us on a compelling mystical journey from her birth, to marriage, to liberation, her ultimate expulsion and beyond.

Moving past her biblical relationship with Adam and her dismissal from Eden, Lilith emerges in later texts as the wife of the Angel Samael. Her marriage to him evokes the counterparts of Adam to Eve. The thought-provoking and dark Treatise on the Left Emanation written by Rabbi Isaac ben Jacob ha-Kohen in the first half of the thirteenth century introduces Lilith and the angel Samael as wife and husband, a concept which was then incorporated into later Kabbalistic demonology.

> Truly I shall give you a hint, that the reason for all the jealousies which exist between the princes mentioned above, and the [other, good] princes which belong to the seven classes, the classes of the holy angels which are called "the guardians of the walls," the reason which evokes hatred and jealousy between the heavenly powers and the powers of the supreme host, is one form which is destined for Samael, and it is Lilith, and it has the image of a feminine form, and Samael is in the form of Adam and Lilith in the form of Eve. Both of them were born in a spiritual birth as one, similar to the form of Adam and Eve, like two pairs of twins, one above and one below. Samael and the Eve the Elder, which is called the Northern one, they are emanated from below the Throne of Glory, and this was caused by the Sin.[21]

> They say that from Asmodeus and his mate Lilith a great prince was born in heaven. He is the ruler of eighty thousand destructive demons and is called "the sword of king Asmodeus." His name is Alefpene'ash and His face burns like a raging fire ('esh). He is also called Gurigur, for he antagonizes and struggles with the prince of Judah, who is called Gur Aryeh Yehudah (Lion-cub of Judah). From the same form that gave birth to this war-demon another prince, a prince whose root is in Kingdom, was born in heaven. He is called "the sword of the Messiah." He too has two names: Meshihi'el and Kokhvi'el. When the time comes and when God wishes, this sword will leave its sheath and verses of prophecy will come True: "For My sword shall be drunk

in the heavens; Lo, it shall come down upon Edom" (Isaiah 34:5). "A star rises from Jacob" (Numbers; 24:17). Amen. Soon in our days may we merit to see the face of the Messiah our righteous one; we and all our people ...[22]

The angel Samael is also important in Kabbalah. Scholem shows (in *The Origins of the Kabbalah*) that in early medieval Kabbalah, Samael retained some of the characteristics of the Gnostic demiurge Ialdebaoth (the blind god), and derives the name from "sami," meaning "blind." He is attributed consistently to the planet Mars and the sephira Gevurah, and is the source of all the nastiness in the world. He appears in various guises as the Dark Angel and the Angel of Death. The suffix -el betrays his divine origin, and Kabbalists have been divided between placing him at the head of a demonic hierarchy (alongside his wife Lilith), and viewing him as an unpleasant but necessary component of creation. Samael is identified with the serpent in the Garden of Eden, a tempter and a poisoner of life.[23]

Continuing from the Treatise on the Left Emanation #18 we get multiple references to Lilith in her guise as the wife of Samuel as listed on this site: (http://jewishchristianlit.com/Topics/Lilith/jacob_ha_kohen.html).

What does the tale of Lilith really represent to our own current civilization? She was the hidden mythological prototype of the first woman whose sexuality blazed hot and who neither Adam nor God could handle or should I say tame! Is she simply another myth about a so-called fallen woman or does she represent something more profound, something deeper? Until recently and throughout most "history" there had only ever been two accepted courses laid out for women: one to be quiet, submissive and virginal, and therefore "good" or to be sexually free-spirited, independent thinking, thus being labeled "bad," the latter most often resulting in dire consequences. In the spirit of Lilith, millions of women throughout the ages were put to death in many hideous ways from horrid tortures, to drowning or hanging or burning at the stake. Why, because they did not toe the line, but chose to question the established order, they claimed their powers, their intelligence and their feminine strengths and thus paid a heavy price.

As a proud Witch, High Priestess, Sacred Temple and Ritual Dancer, it is my opinion and hopefully that of others that Lilith represents the personification of a strong, independent and intelligent Goddess in touch with the powers of her Sacred Feminine mystic. Lilith knew what she was about, she didn't accept the fate that was handed out to her, she tried to change that fate for her betterment. She was a risk taker who challenged unjust authority and won. Yes, she won because she did attain her freedom.

Now, suddenly, Lilith is back. Her image and story have made a revival appearance in our culture, from magazines to the internet, she is becoming a trendy icon and she is everywhere. Times have changed with women in many modern cultures finally re-claiming their status and embracing the ancient image of the Sacred Feminine.

Yet I still find comfort in searching for Lilith's true essence in the ancient texts. To quote a passage in Genesis I:27: "So God created man in his own Image, in the Image of God created he him; male and female created he them." Again, we have an example that clearly states the fact that there was a first female created alongside a first male. A female who was created equal, the one we know as Lilith. So why not act like an equal? Lilith did just that.

Yet Genesis continues without another mention of the first female. She seems to have disappeared. What did the reality of Lilith's departure mean to Adam? Was he weakened, embarrassed, distraught? Ancient mythological texts after all do hint that many of these hypotheses are seen as truth. The lesson here seems to go beyond the fact that Adam couldn't control his living situation or his first mate. What does all this say about Adam's sexual prowess, if Lilith wouldn't lie beneath him? Did Adam ever get over losing Lilith? After all, his desire for her was never really satisfied. Is that why our patriarchal forefathers created the mythological tale about the desirable Lilith, the seductress, temptress of the night, even referenced as possibly God's consort? What powerful symbolism of fear does that represent? Nighttime darkness when men sleep and are most vulnerable Lilith comes, the succubus and ... Is the story of Lilith built upon certain male insecurities!

To understand Lilith is to accept her persona as a woman who is in touch with her sexuality and its power. Though Adam's story and the rest of this particular very ancient mythology seems to conclude with Lilith's demonizing, it is nothing less than a story of fate. For her fate pushes aside her demon qualities and applauds her as a strong sexually independent female. The Bible mentions other such females, one is the Queen of Sheba who as a seductive temptress and sorceress, is referenced in association with Lilith.

Once again the serpent as a well-known ancient symbol of the Goddess and messenger of the Divine Feminine snakes through "history." Quoting from the Kabbalah:

And the Serpent, the Woman of Harlotry, incited and seduced Eve through the husks of Light which in itself is holiness. And the Serpent seduced Holy Eve, and enough said for him who understands. An all this ruination came about because Adam the first man coupled with Eve while she was in her menstrual impurity – this is the filth and the impure seed of the Serpent who mounted Eve before Adam mounted her. Behold, here it is before you: because of the sins of Adam the first man all the things mentioned came into being. For Evil

Lilith, when she saw the greatness of his corruption, became strong in her husks, and came to Adam against his will, and became hot from him and bore him many demons and spirits and Lilin.[24]

Women who are in touch with their sexual allure and power, women who thirst for knowledge and women who use that knowledge, these so-called harlots, prostitutes and whores joined millions of their sisters and were burned or stoned, drowned or simply demonized. And let us not forget the other independent thinking women, the village cunning women and the healing midwives who also shared these tortures, because their ancient herbs and potions cured the sick and their hands helped bring the gift of life safely into the world. Redheaded, blond, brunette, black haired, grey and white we hold the mystery, we are all desirable, and thus all necessary to control. If women cease to let the images of these wrongs influence their behavior and allow themselves to reclaim the potent essence of Lilith, we would be reminded of what could have been and what could still be. It is the Goddess in each of us.

In Queen Mary's Psalter (1553) one sees a delicate painting of Lilith pictured with a beautiful face, abundant tresses and the body of a cat. Created by a British artist in the fourteenth century, this small miniature painting is a potent interpretative artist's image of Lilith to medieval civilization. Perhaps the myth of the black cat as a familiar to witches had its origin with this painting. With the feminine symbol of the sensuous black cat always so sleek and graceful in its movements, no wonder tales ran rampant of "evil omens" (which signify fear of the unknown) if such a cat crossed one's path.

There are two animal creatures associated with Lilith. One we are familiar with as the snaking apple temptress of the "garden" and the other is the Night Owl. The most famous picture of Lilith (depicting her as the Owl) and a personal favorite of mine comes from "The Lilith Relief" which is a Sumerian terra-cotta relief (circa 2000–1600 BCE known as the Burney Relief – after the original owner Mr. Sydney Burney who came to own this relief in 1936). Lilith is depicted as a beautiful winged woman whose ring and staff have been interpreted as justice. Her owl claws represent the owl's nocturnal flight. The relief is topped off with Lilith's seductive snake-like flowing and unbound hair which I interpret as crowning her Divinity and defining her Sacred Femininity. Lilith transcends all that went before by this most riveting image. (A copy of this plaque majestically rests upon my altar.)

Thus, Lilith in her screech owl persona joins her sisters: Hecate Goddess of the Crossroads and the night owl and the Welsh Goddess Blodeuwedd who was punished and turned into an owl after being unfaithful. Thus the night owl becomes another symbol of the mysterious, the darkness and the unknown and thus a symbol of the feared Divine Feminine.

Here we come to another of Lilith's many and far reaching evolutions and my favorite, her transition into the image of the powerful Crone, also the night hag of the succubus world, who embodies our fears of the unknown, of death and of change. The Dark Goddess who as Lilith and her Sisters became unjustly transformed into the wicked, the untamed, the feared, the seducers, the destroyers and takers of life. They are Queens of the realms of darkness, ruling the void of moon days. Their strong natures rule over Magick, mystery, sexual power, and all worldly accomplishments. The mature and beautiful Crone in the guise of Lilith represents independence, great knowledge and the wisdom of life's experience. She is the Wise One.

Lilith (Lili, Lilin. Lillake, Lilite. Lillet, Lamia) Temptress, Leader and Wise Woman, Goddess of the unknown you represent to your daughters the fundamental strength and determination of opportunity, freedom and sexual power and the attainment of knowledge. Sacred Divinity lives on in her image. And as Her spiritual offspring we must remember our roots and we must remember Her.

Endnotes

1. http://www.ecauldron.net/kabbalah.php;
2. http://addictionssophiaofwisdom3cek.tripod.com/id29.html
3. Genesis 1:20–21
4. Zohar i. 34b
5. Yalqut Reubeni to Genesis 2:21, p.68
6. Zohar iii 19b
7. Zohar i. 148a Sitre Torah, Wayne State University Press, 3rd edition, 1978
8. *The* Alphabet of ben Sira http://jewishchristianlit.com/Topics/Lilith/bible.html
9. *The Hebrew Goddess*, p. 240 Raphael Patai,
10. Zohar 19a.

11. https://www.biblicalarchaeology.org/daily/people-cultures-in-the-bible/people-in-the-bible/lilith/
12. http://www.sria.org/lilith-the-demon/
13. From *Revelation and other Prophetic Books of the Bible*, St. John the Evangelist and Others; Dover Publications Inc. Mineola, NY
14. From *New English Bible New Testament*, Oxford University Press, Cambridge University Press 1961
16. Dictionary.com Unabridged (v.1.1) Based on the Random House Unabridged Dictionary, c Random House Inc. 2006
16. http://www.asphodel-long.com/html/lilith.html
17. http://altreligion.about.com/library/glossary/bldefsuccubus.htm
18. http://www.atomick.net/fayelevine/pk/demons/pk003.php
19. http://www.asphodel-long.com/html/lilith.html
20. http://www.sria.org/lilith-the-demon/
21. 'Treatise on the Left Emanation' from Chapter 6
22. 'Treatise on the Left Emanation' #19
23. http://www.digital-brilliance.com/kab/faq.htm
24. Kabbalah Bacharach, 'Emeq haMelekh 23c-d

Chapter 3

Eve: Birth of the First "Wife"

The divorce of Lilith and Adam was final.

"And the Lord God caused a deep sleep to fall upon Adam, and he slept; and he took one of his ribs, and closed up the flesh instead thereof. And the rib which the Lord God had taken from man, made he a woman, and brought her unto the man." And Adam said, "This is now bone of my bones, and flesh of my flesh; she shall be called Woman, because she was taken out of Man."[1] "And Adam called his wife's name Eve, because she was the mother of all living."[2]

Adam was now alone and Lilith would soon be replaced with the second choice. The first "wife" was created to remedy the ills of the first "partner," or so it was thought! As history dictated the memory of the first partner, Lilith was destined to be relegated to the hidden archives as a lesson. As the ancient story unfolds, since Eve was formed out of Adam's rib, she was not his equal. Now there would be no doubt of her dependence, and the embarrassing question of feminine rights might never be raised again.

Let us continue with the story of the woman who replaced Lilith in biblical mythology and numerous ancient texts. Sweet demure Eve at first seemed the perfect wife. Created as she was from Adam's rib, she was guaranteed to be the lesser. What happiness was there for Adam after the debacle of Lilith? This time he would surely get the control and order he deserved. Or so he thought!

Lilith and Eve were each created for the same original purpose, to satisfy Adam and not question authority. Though created/born at different times, each was touched by the male God in his unique moment of procreation. They were genetically birthed to be similar in physicality yet dissimilar in their spirit. Perhaps the seductive scent of Lilith lingered on his fingers as God knowingly or perhaps unknowingly passed the strong genetic seed of Lilith to Eve. They were and are sisters under the skin.

If life in this so called biblical paradise or Garden of Eden was really so wonderful and suited to both Adam and Eve's needs, temptation would never have come into play. Why then would the seductive serpent coiled around a tree need to tempt at all? The male God supposedly created all, including the tempestuous serpent. The serpent was not a mistake. I see this as the ultimate planned temptation to create the ideal transgression. Should we read between biblical lines or question the authority of such words? Yes, because if God is supposed to be all knowing and perfectly good why the need to create an atmosphere whereby distrust and disobedience even exist? Certainly, we can guess this lesson!

On that premise we've been taught that God had a very intricate master plan to teach humanity lessons. I am sure Divinity did, but I tend to believe that the biblical writers wrote and manipulated this story of Adam, Lilith and Eve to suit their patriarchal purpose. How perfect to generate a God given story that would form the dogma of authoritarian rule allowing mankind the ability to maintain order, but most importantly to control the Feminine mystic.

Now the serpent was craftier than any of the wild animals the LORD God had made. He said to the woman, "Did God really say, 'You must not eat from any tree in the garden'?"

The woman said to the serpent, "We may eat fruit from the trees in the garden, but God did say, 'You must not eat fruit from the tree that is in the middle of the garden, and you must not touch it, or you will die.'"

"You will not surely die," the serpent said to the woman.

"For God knows that when you eat of it your eyes will be opened, and you will be like God, knowing good and evil."

When the woman saw that the fruit of the tree was good for food and pleasing to the eye, and also desirable for gaining wisdom, she took some and ate it. She also gave some to her husband, who was with her, and he ate it. Then the eyes of both of them were opened, and they realized they were naked; so, they sewed fig leaves together and made coverings for themselves.[3]

Oh, the wonderful yet troublesome serpent, as Lilith in disguise, manifesting its presence to remind Eve of her genetic powers passed from sister to sister. Perhaps God miscalculated. One can change the physical but the soul remains the same!

Curiously we find written: Genesis 2 narrates that "God places the first man and woman in a garden with trees of whose fruits they may eat, but forbids them to eat from 'the tree of the knowledge of good and evil.'" When, in Genesis 3, "a serpent seduces the woman to eat from its forbidden fruit and she also lets the man taste it, God expels them from the garden and thereby from eternal life."[4]

Well that quote certainly omits the fact that Lilith was the first woman!

And was Eve's temptation and subsequently Adams' solely the result of one spiraling serpent or the allure of the abundantly fruitful intertwining tree that offered up such mysteries?

"The tree of the knowledge of good and evil is one of two trees in the story of the Garden of Eden in Genesis 2-3, along with the tree of life. A cylinder seal, known as the temptation seal, from post-Akkadian periods in Mesopotamia (c. 23rd–22nd century BCE), has been linked to the Adam and Eve story."[5]

Fate allowed Eve to be the curious one and to be pulled towards the forbidden knowledge and life held in the fertile tree. And fate also allowed the silky-smooth serpent glowing within and without with colors of green and browns whose warm body hugged the tree to become Eve's friend. As Eve's eyes met the piecing glow of the vibrant yellow serpent's eyes, she was transfixed. Such tempting whispers for her ears alone told the tale of many things. Of now and the future.

Perhaps it was more than the mesmerizing snake or the desire to taste the rich apple that attracted Eve, but the idea of power and independence and of stubborn determination. Let us remember, in the biblical texts Eve was instructed again and again by Adam and her God to remember his rules, her dependence and her lowly status. Although temptation caught Eve first with that succulent bite, Adam was not able to walk away from it. Obviously, there was another side to Eve! And although Adam was created before Eve, he did not show enough strength to resist the serpent's mysterious lure. He took a bite of the luxuriant apple that promised the secrets of untold wisdom. Though not credited with any fault in the deed, Adam followed Eve's leadership and did succumb to temptation. His actions were almost equal to hers but Adam absolutely did not share Eve's fall from grace. She took the full burden.

There is an even more controversial concept as this story continues. After the shame and fall to earth we have the biblical appearance of Eve's earthly sons Cain and Abel and the propagation of their offspring comes into question. After all, if Eve and Adam where biblical parents, then how, dare I ask, was it incestual, Mother to Son, Female to Male? Because the immaculate conception myth did not come until much later.

Poor Eve, whose paradise-shattering action was destined to carry the burden of servitude and pain for all womankind in this all too familiar ancient mythology. Did she perhaps feel the innocent pleasure that was her reward in that one moment when she succumbed to the desirably seductive taste of the apple? Was it really an evil disobedience or simply a need to show her determined independence and passion?

And what of the apple? History has downgraded its significance to a very ordinary fruit. We have the apple cobbler, apple pie and the candied apple, certainly the most family-oriented deserts in existence. Forbidden fruit that has now become mainstream! Yet there is one school of thought amongst many New Age religions, that it wasn't a ripe apple at all but a bright red pomegranate which is believed to be an aphrodisiac. This is reminiscent of the story of Persephone who is tricked and tempted by Hades to taste the pomegranate. Her desire wins over judgment and she is then bound to him forever as winter turns to spring. Both red fruits are round, rich in fullness and juicy.

What is the message in the desire of "forbidden fruit"? Throughout history, politicians and monarchs alike have succumbed to the rewards of tasting the forbidden fruits of women. There were the wives and then the forbidden delights of concubines, mistresses, prostitutes and harems. The fruits of power and wealth have driven men to war again and again, annihilating entire civilizations in an effort to maintain that taste. The patriarchal God mustn't mind wars and killing so very much because that seems nothing compared to the horrid taint of innocent Eve's biting the tempestuous apple as the creator of the "original sin."

I ask, in this lush Garden of Eden why was anything forbidden at all, unless there really was a deliberate calculated plan. Adam already beaten down from his previous marital experiences with Lilith certainly wouldn't rock the boat of complacency. Eve on the other hand was the sister of Lilith and she had the inherited genetic spark of strength which gave her the ability to question and to attain desire. In my opinion, it is a lot less volatile to bite an apple than to declare war.

Original Sin ... what is that really? Is it a myth whereby the so-called first wife disobeys the rules and authority created by the male God? It's not very "original" since Lilith's supposed disobedience and damnation came before Eve's! Yet women throughout the ages have suffered incredible indignities from Eve's story. Here is a myth that became so powerful that Lilith slips to the wayside in demon obscurity to make way for Eve's evil universal renown. It is a myth with a sole purpose to prejudge and pre-punish all women, just in case. The patriarchal "religious" taste for power was not to be toyed with!

I was recently at a viewing for a dear friend's mother who passed away. Since my friend's mother was Catholic, a Deacon from her parish church came to give a blessing over the coffin. But instead of the simple comforting blessing everyone expected, this male Deacon began a tirade on "original sin" and how my friend's mother "this woman" carried the yoke of Eve's original sin, as do all women. This so-called man of the church went on to describe how my friend's mother tried to rise above this "sin" by becoming a good mother and wife, and how wonderful that now in death, she was free of its hold.

I was appalled and so was my friend's family with such a negative and unworthy speech about a dear mother and grandmother who was anything but a "sinner." How naïve I felt at that moment when I remembered, what I had thought was a truth, that archaic attitudes about women had totally died down with the right to vote in 1920 and the call to equal rights and feminism in the 1970s. How wrong I was.

There is fear in the all-powerful Sacred Feminine. Sadly, throughout the centuries since the patriarchal religions took over, women have been taught to disregard any empowered instincts that they may have for the more docile instinct of a subservient creature. The average women's role for centuries had been one of tending the home and birthing the children. Though both are noble occupations, women were not encouraged to be free-thinkers, because that was reserved for men. Many of us grew up believing the myth of Eve and were taught to feel guilt, blame and shame. I ask for what? Is it for daring to feel deserving of what we want and truly merit? Times have and are continuously changing. The Goddess has made a substantial re-emergence and many areas of our planet are experiencing renewed balance from the Goddess. Though regretfully, so many cultures are still in the Dark Ages with women's issues. I and many others of like mind believe that, through a slow process, the energy of Goddess and the Sacred Feminine are returning to balance our world.

Even as a small child, who felt she was destined to become a Catholic Nun, I did not ascribe to Eve's negative myth. Somehow or other I held the formidable inner belief that as a female I was special. Perhaps at the time I unknowingly inherited the thread that bound me to Divinity and the Goddess as Lilith.

Women are passionate and their sexuality has an innate power and if some men cannot control their urges, we certainly can. That is what gives us power over them. And for that we have been punished and tortured throughout history. Why, I ask, were the unwed mother and the adulteress stoned to death and the whore condemned? Are their male counterparts ever punished, not to my knowledge? It hasn't even been that long in the course of human existence that men are acknowledged as having sperm that definitely plays a part in reproduction. Before this discovery it was guilt again and again because it was thought to be entirely the woman's fault if she did not conceive or produce the needed male offspring. I never cease to be amazed at the vast amount of historical and scientific hype and falsehoods that have been passed off as truth and reality!

One day I walked into a chocolatier's shop and was beguiled by a delicious confection aptly entitled "Eve." The confection's smooth outside was of fine dark Belgium chocolate with a pure vanilla truffle cream center. Was Eve's pure white vanilla interior really a ploy for a decadent exterior? Certainly, Eve's so called biblical disobedience meant that she had a risky, unruly and perhaps a little unpredictable side. Certainly, it wasn't worthy of taking upon herself and all of womankind the overwhelming burden of guilt and blame. If the world is not paradise it is not because of Eve, it is because of war, destruction, rape and pillage, which throughout history can be mostly blamed on patriarchal religious fervor and hierarchy. The early Christian male Popes were very guilty of such desirable greed and power. Their followers tortured and killed again and again during the Crusades and the Inquisition in the name of their male God. The Popes, so revered by the Catholics, supposedly adhered to the strict vows of celibacy laid out by the Apostle Peter. It is well documented that they were mostly otherwise! Throughout history there is definite proof that many so called "infallible" Popes kept both male and female lovers, plus numerous wives and mistresses, and fathered plenty of children, all the while preaching abstinence and holding strict dynastic power over the life and death of their many subjects. When I think of history, both then and now, I am sickened by the continuous tales of bloodshed in the name of a peaceful and pure God. What kind of God would condone, much less allow, such atrocities of torture and destruction in his name?

The name Eve is derived from the Hebrew word which means *living*, or *life giver*, and by extension, *mother*. While all subsequent "biblical cultures" have Eve as an ancestor, she is unique in that although all people after her were physically created from woman, Eve herself was created from a man. How convenient was this mythological biblical story to the ancient patriarchal strategy? I would rather think of myself as descended from the purely feminine and equal Lilith line!

So, if biblically speaking Eve is thought to be our ancestor, what does that make Lilith? Born first, her genetic thread was woven into her younger sister Eve's persona and she reappears in many incarnations as a constant reminder. Was the serpent, again playing its part in "Herstory" so desirous and alluring, an embodiment of Lilith that came to remind Eve of her genetic connection to her sister? The Sistine Chapel holds a painting where Lilith is portrayed as the serpent as do many other ancient religious paintings. She has often been portrayed by artists as having a beautiful head, long tresses and naked upper body with her lower torso in the form of a serpent. The image reminds me of the mysterious Mermaid. As Sirens of the watery depths, Mermaids have been fantasized in poems and writings as the personification of the female seductress!

"Now the serpent was more crafty than any of the wild animals the LORD God had made. He said to the woman, 'Did God really say, "You must not eat from any tree in the garden"?'."[6]

Did Lilith beguile the serpent that guarded the gates of Eden and mimic its form just to tempt/remind Eve of her genetic heritage? Here we have Eve in her one moment of enlightenment which aligns her to her sister Lilith's myth in that both acted against the male authoritative rule unjustly imposed upon them. Mirror images of each other, we have Lilith sensuous, bold and determined not to be enslaved and we have Eve balking at unfair authority obviously biased towards man. Eve embraced her temptation by savoring that brief moment of a deliciously tasty apple bite. With her story moving from her fall to the expulsion from the garden, we have Eve bravely dealing with the consequences of life after Eden. It wasn't the yoke of her "original sin" that Eve had to endure, but the yoke of Adam tied to her through the promise of future generations of patriarchal judgment and dominance.

So, for the Eves of this world who have endured and now awakened to their genetic destiny within the powerful Sacred Feminine, temptation is just another word for enticement, attraction, allure or appeal. From temptation comes temptress.

Endnotes

1. Genesis 2:22; 23 & 24
2. Genesis 3:20

3. Genesis 3
4. en.wikipedia.org/wiki/Tree_of_the_knowledge_of_good_
   and_evil
5. en.wikipedia.org/wiki/Tree_of_the_knowledge_of_good_
   and_evil
6. Genesis 3:1 http://www.biblestudytools.com/dictionary/ser
   pent/

Chapter 4

Sisters under the Skin: The Priestess and the Sacred Prostitute?

To better understand the impact that the Sacred Divinities of the Feminine religions had on pre and post Christian societies, one must recognize not only the mystical awe that the Goddess once held for the populace, but the reverence and respect of her earthly counterparts the Temple Priestesses, and their sacred and perhaps sexual duties. As predecessors and successors to Lilith and Eve, the Priestesses' long reign spanned every culture and era to influence and enhance the worship and beliefs of many different ancient societies. Though it is the male Temple Priest of antiquity who seems to dominate most documented references, the myth and memory of his female complement beckons. The Temple of Apollo in Greece housed one well-known Priestess, the Prophetess or Oracle of Delphi, the Pythia. Regretfully, her visionary powers were too often credited to the inspiration of Apollo.

> The most relevant example being Cassandra, daughter of Priam and Hecuba of Troy, who, like the Pythia is described as being "possessed" by Apollo, while she uttered her oracles in a kind of frenzy. The only difference was that Cassandra's prophecies were destined never to be believed. Perhaps then, the only influence on the Pythia's state was the affect of the pneuma (the "soul" or "vital spirit," often associated in antiquity with a vapor), not as a toxic gas, but as the divine wisdom or breath of Apollo.[1]

The Priestesses not only studied the mysteries, worshipped a Deity or Deities while performing religious rites in their honor, but were the human interpreters of the Sacred Feminine divine principles, thus becoming the spiritual advisors to their followers.

Some draped their heads in white wool veils as the Vestal Virgins of Ancient Rome while the Priestesses of the Egyptian Goddess Isis wore soft flowing white draped tunics. There is one school of thinkers which feels that virtually every ancient Goddess-worshipping culture from Sumeria and Mesopotamia, to Egypt and Babylonia, Rome and Greece, Crete and India to the Celtic lands all housed temples with an honored Priestess class.

In the ancient Near East, women could in fact be dedicated by their fathers or their masters to a deity. Women could also devote themselves to the service of a god or a goddess in order to secure their living. This was done mainly by young widows without grown children, by repudiated wives, by female slaves sent away (like Hagar, Abraham's concubine in Genesis 21), by lonely women, etc. These "consecrated" persons performed tasks in the sanctuary, provided domestic help in temple annexes, perhaps provided musical entertainment and possibly sexual services, remitting their fees to the temple.[2]

It is within this Priestess class that women could achieve power in cultures that otherwise did not hold women as important. But did these spiritual women channel their chosen Goddess in a unique commingle of Divinity plus sexuality? Is it such a difficult concept to comprehend? Does it always need to be debated and argued as to the mere possibility? The idea or reality of a Priestess in the guise of a "Divine Wife" or Sacred Prostitute seems nothing more than the definition of an enlightened woman who embraces her spiritualty within her sexuality as she channels the revered missive of the Goddess.

She allows this celestial ecstasy to fill her spiritual and physical being. If she really did exist and was more than an illusion or fictional myth, this Sacred Prostitute would have initiated the Divine union between earthly man and herself as representative of the Sacrosanct. Within the aura of her mystical awareness she would have become the architect of pleasure in that partnership between Feminine Divinity and man. It would and can be the powerful melding of the Goddess and the God.

Though the controversy persists between scholars and historians, there are numerous historical references that help to outline the plausibility of the Temple Prostitute.

Religious prostitution, sacred prostitution or temple prostitution is the practice of having sexual intercourse (with a person other than one's spouse) for a religious or sacred purpose. A woman engaged in such practices is sometimes called a temple prostitute or hierodule, though modern connotations of the term prostitute may or may not be appropriate, given the religious and cultic signification of the activities.[3]

Sacred prostitution, temple prostitution, cult prostitution, and religious prostitution are general terms for a sexual ritual consisting of sexual intercourse or other sexual activity performed in the context of religious worship, perhaps as a form of fertility rite or divine marriage. Some scholars prefer the term sacred sex to sacred prostitution in cases where payment for services was not involved.[4]

In Sumer and later in Babylon, religious rituals involved sacred sexuality in the form of the Sacred Marriage or hieros gamos, an act simulating marriage between the fertility goddess Inanna/Ishtar and the shepherd god, Dumuzi. In this act, the high priestess of Inanna would have intercourse with either the high priest or the king of the city. Through the sexual act, divine fertile energy was released on the land ensuring good crops and productive herds. Sacred prostitution involved temple priestesses of Inanna/Ishtar having ritual sex with male visitors to the temple, again releasing the divine fertile energy. Both of these sacred sexual practices existed for thousands of years in Mesopotamia. It is best to understand these rituals as a religious act of devotion to the goddess rather than as sex per se. After all, secular prostitutes plied their trade in Mesopotamian cities as well.[5]

Has the fine line between the possible role of the Temple Priestess and that of the Sacred Prostitute been smudged?

In Greece, the goddess Cotytto was a guardian of prostitutes; and most famous are the priestesses of Aphrodite – several times named as goddess of prostitutes – and her temple in Corinth (Greece); a city famous for its legions of both sacred and secular prostitutes. On the island of Cyprus, too, the temples of Aphrodite were served by such women. Farther west, among the Romans, we find sacred hierodules on the Italian mainland and in Sicily; with the goddesses Acca Larentia and Venus being thus worshipped.[6]

In the book *When God Was a Woman* Merlin Stone states that the Hebrew word "zonah" means both prostitute and prophetess.

"The only passage of the Bible referring possibly to cult prostitution is 2 Kings 23:7, that refers to 'women renting houses as a shrine', but its text is often 'corrected' and mistranslated."[7]

Perhaps there have been many famous "prostitutes" of antiquity and beyond, but none more famous than the New Testament biblical temptress and later Saint of the long-unbound tresses, the "hetaira" Mary Magdalene. She first appears in Luke 8:13 as a follower of Jesus named Mary, called Magdalene.

It was said of Jesus:

During his journey, he was visited by two women, the unnamed sinner in Luke 7 and Mary of Bethany, both of whom anoint his feet and dry them with their hair, similar to the way Magdalene anointed him shortly after his death. In 591, Pope Gregory the Great stated that all three were in fact one woman, Mary Magdalene, and this is how she became labeled as a prostitute, or the unnamed sinner. However, the Second Vatican Council removed the prostitute label in 1969 after much debate and Biblical evidence that there was more than one Mary and that Mary of Magdalene and the unnamed sinner were two different figures.[8]

An interesting fact that I uncovered was that the Actress Anita Stinger Dacanay wrote and performed a play about Mary Magdalene entitled "Oadishtu" a word that means "holy women." And these "holy women" usually resided in temples.

I truly believe Mary Magdalene, so imbued with legend, was a Temple Priestess and Sacred Prostitute. Though the debate is still on and very heated, perhaps the other Mary, the Madonna was in fact a Temple Priestess also and her immaculate conception began as none other than her channeling the Goddess with a sacred union. The idea of this within any Christian faith is unimaginable and sacra religious. Yet to others, this concept is very conceivable.

If allowed to be herself, perhaps Lilith would have been the more famous Sacred Prostitute with a following of Temple Priestesses that regularly channeled Divinity. If that was ever a possibility of being a mythological reality, history has certainly deleted any probable reference to such an outcome.

No matter how the historical press misinterpreted and demeaned their role, many of our ancestors saw the Priestess as essential and blessed and when their ritual of sacred communion was performed they offered earthly participants the ability to see, feel and touch Divinity. Did she join in the sanctified rite of copulation that some ancient civilizations believed would ensure the good health and welfare of the community, welcoming fertile and abundant crops? Were they the spiritual wives or handmaidens to their Deity? To many ancient Goddess-worshipping people the act of commingling with Divinity through a Temple Priestess was not only an honor of great reverence but was looked upon as vital to the well-being of everyone both spiritually and bodily. What better way to honor the Sacred Feminine Deity than to join her in sacred union whether in actual ritual or symbolic. I believe as many do, that this Temple Priestess held a place of awe in the community. As an unmarried (symbolically or actually virginal) woman living apart from the community, she was thus free to become enlightened in her thinking and choices. The thread of Lilith's persona of free-thinking independence mixed with Eve's willingness to copulate traveled through the ages.

On certain seasonal occasions and celebrations many ancient cultures chose a Priestess who would go into deep meditation to attune with the Goddess and channel her powers. This powerful energy would enable the special Priestess who was often selected at birth to be raised in the temple and trained in the ancient mysteries, to make predictions. She was the seer and sage, the revered one who channeled the Divine source into her own body to become the earthly representative of the Sacred Feminine as the Goddess herself. She possessed the telepathic and intuitive skills that set her apart. She encompassed all Divinity within the seductive Lilith, the all-powerful Isis, the wise Hecate and the motherly and nurturing Eve. Is it fact or fiction that beyond predictions this most revered Temple Priestess had a second and equally powerful role as a Sacred Prostitute of Antiquity?

There is one holiday in the ancient pre-Christian and Pagan eras that above all held the Sacred Prostitute in her guise as

Temple Priestess in definite awe. The first of May or May Day, when the modern world parades their power and might, was to those of ancient pagan times the Rites of Spring or to the Celts the feast of "Beltaine."

> It was a time to honor fertility with unbridled merrymaking, when young and old would spend the night making love in the green woods. In the morning, they would return to their villages bearing huge budding boughs of hawthorn (the may-tree) and other spring flowers with which to bedeck themselves, their families, and their houses. They would procession back home, stopping at each house to leave flowers, and enjoy the best of food and drink that the home had to offer. In every village, the maypole—usually a birch or ash pole—was raised, and dancing and feasting began. Festivities were led by the May Queen and her consort, the King who was sometimes Jack-in-the-Green, or the Green Man, the old god of the wildwood. They were borne in state through the village in a cart covered with flowers and enthroned in a leafy arbor as the divine couple whose unity symbolized the sacred marriage of earth and sun.[9]

Fertility rites are religious rituals that reenact, either actually or symbolically, sexual acts and/or reproductive processes: "sexual intoxication is a typical component of the ... rites of the various functional gods who control reproduction, whether of man, beast, cattle, or grains of seed."[10]

Mystical and Corporeal rituals defined the Sacred Feminine to our ancient ancestors and brought the Divinity of each civilization's Matron Goddess down to the earthly human realm. Ancient myths tell tales of how it was vital and very important for a new ruler as King or Emperor to participate and thus secure his reign in a sacred ritualistic wedding. During this ceremony it was expected that he would copulate with the Temple Priestess who represented the Goddess. Thereby he would receive the Divine sovereignty of governance. Their sacred marital union was a gift of absolute heredity, power that passed through the Divine Goddess to the Priestess and given to the sovereign as the representative of the earthly God.

One undervalued Priestess story is that of Hypatia of Alexandria, the Priestess and Librarian of the Library at Alexandria. Her story has been dramatized throughout history to portray a woman who would not stand down from her pagan and scholarly beliefs. She saw the world through a philosopher and mathematician's eyes. This was very unique to women of pre-Christian times. She was a woman of great intelligence mixed with regal beauty. To defend the Library (temple), she sacrificed her life thus proving her passionate beliefs. She was a product of the "old" during a time when the idea of the Sacred Feminine was being removed from thought. Her intensity was powerful. She was an intellectual leader, yet history focuses in great detail on her beauty. Is there another story here? After all, she did thoroughly enthrall her students. Nonetheless, she was brutally murdered for her female "stubbornness." "History" is never fair.

The term Priestess can be defined and interpreted within many forms. Catholic nuns to this day participate in a symbolic marriage to their "God." At the petition for their final vow of "perpetual profession" they begin to wear a gold wedding band and call themselves "brides" of Christ. Once again, we have a revered ancient custom morphing into a Christian tradition with its meaning transferred to the patriarch's God. But the mysticism and the seclusion of the Nuns' lives mimic a sort of "temple" where women live, worship and give themselves to a Deity.

Though the role of the Priestess has changed as she traveled through the millennia, she is still with us.

Modern Wicca or Paganism and Witchcraft have brought us a new class of Priestess. Within each modern coven (a group or gathering of witches who meet regularly), is a Priestess or High Priestess who channels the Goddess at various times within ritual. She works alongside and yet apart from the Coven Priest. But times have changed and the idea of a "sacred union" within a coven has simply morphed into nothing more than a "symbolic act or ritual," or has it?

It has been estimated that the number of Americans that are Wiccans is doubling every 30 months, and at this point there are more than 200,000 registered witches and approximately 8 million unregistered practitioners of Wicca. And it is important to remember that Wicca is just one form of witchcraft. There are many other "darker" forms of witchcraft that are also experiencing tremendous growth.[11]

Was the original premise of the alliance between Lilith and Adam and later Lilith and the Angel Samael meant to symbolize not only the sexual, but the spiritual connection between the Goddess and God, two halves of Divinity's whole? Was Lilith, so close to her creator, meant to be our first Sacred Prostitute?

Endnotes

1. http://www.ancient.eu/article/205/
2. (Edward Lipiński, "Cult Prostitution in Ancient Israel?" Biblical Archaeology Review, January/February 2014.) https://members.bib-arch.org/biblical-archaeology-review/40/1
3. Stephanie Budin, *The Myth of Sacred Prostitution in Antiquity* (Cambridge University Press, 2009); see also the book review by Vinciane Pirenne-Delforge, Bryn Mawr Classical Review, April 28, 2009;.www.Wikepedia.com
4. https://en.wikipedia.org/wiki/Sacred_prostitution
5. https://www.historyonthenet.com/sacred-marriage-and-sacred-prostitution-in-ancient-mesopotamia/

6. http://www.yoniversum.nl/dakini/ritprost.html
7. Cult Prostitution and Passage Rites in the Biblical World, Edward Lipinski https://www.scribd.com/document/2840 40458/Cult-Prostitution-and-Passage-Rites-in-the-Biblical-World
8. http://departments.kings.edu/womens_history/marymag da.html
9. (taken in part from – www.chalicecentre.net/beltaine.htm)
10. (Max Weber, *The Sociology of Religion* (London 1965) p. 236)
11. http://thetruthwins.com/archives/the-fastest-growing-religion-in-america-is-witchcraft (Quoting from Wikipedia.)

Chapter 5

Lilith's Daughters: The Spiral Dance of the Serpent Goddess

The serpent or snake is one of the oldest and most widespread mythological symbols. The word is derived from Latin *serpens*, a crawling animal or snake. Snakes have been associated with some of the oldest rituals known to humankind and represent dual expression of good and evil.

In some cultures, snakes were fertility symbols. For example, the Hopi people of North America performed an annual snake dance to celebrate the union of Snake Youth (a Sky spirit) and Snake Girl (an Underworld spirit) and to renew the fertility of Nature. During the dance, live snakes were handled and at the end of the dance the snakes were released into the fields to guarantee good crops. "The snake dance is a prayer to the spirits of the clouds, the thunder and the lightning, that the rain may fall on the growing crops." In other cultures, snakes symbolized the umbilical cord, joining all humans to Mother Earth. The Great Goddess often had snakes as her familiars—sometimes twining around her sacred staff, as in ancient Crete—and they were worshiped as guardians of her mysteries of birth and regeneration.[1]

Ah, the fearsome yet seductive image of the Serpent or Snake, one of the oldest and most prevalent mythological symbols of the Feminine archetype crawls through each millennium as a central theme in many Goddess personas. Many ancient societies worshiped this creature as the mysterious guardian of death and regeneration, good and evil. Thus, the ancient Feminine hierarchy embraced this symbol as a central theme in many of their Goddess personas.

Lilith, the Goddess whose image was purposefully suppressed, still intertwined herself into our psyche as the familiar seductive apple temptress of the "Garden." Immortal in her powerful myth she gave birth to her Daughters, Serpent Goddesses of every culture and civilization.

Though the primordial influence of the Serpent Goddesses was once widespread they now, in our time, remained mostly unfamiliar to many. They don't stand alongside the well-known myths of Venus or Diana. Their images are scarce with sometimes pieced together legends, yet they hold us in awe whenever we choose to encounter them. As with Lilith, they are no longer hidden or lost from our view, but are making a resurgence.

Since I have always gravitated towards the shrouded, I have chosen to bring forth the most obscure Serpent Goddesses who define Lilith's sexual serpentine traits. Let them see light.

The mysterious Cretan-Minoan Snake Goddess, who is also a Moon Goddess, is a perfect example of Lilith's enigmatic materialization. Her magnificent image reveals her bared breasts, tiny waist, and elaborately pleated, bell-shaped skirt. She is topped with an intricate coiffure of curled tresses and with arms outstretched, holds a coiling snake in each hand.

The Cretan Priestesses channeled their powerful Goddess completely by mimicking her ornate style of dress and intertwining snake-like hairstyle. Along with the Cretans, these Priestesses worshipped the shedding Serpent as a symbol of the mystifying Moon whose cycle slowly grew to fullness and then died each month. Over and over again the cycle repeated as their Goddess boldly waved Lilith's Serpentine power in her hands for all to view. Was it Lilith saying … "here I am"? Or was it simply a more complicated conundrum in the fact that history has so little "accurate" information about "herstory."

The slithering movements of Snakes can be truly mesmerizing. At a Women's Dark of the Moon Circle long ago I noticed what I thought was an interesting bracelet on one of my Coven initiate's wrists. To my amazement it was a very young boa constrictor who had pneumonia and needed the warmth and comfort of her friend. The little creature held on so timidly! As the little creature regained her health and started to grow, I felt the special joy that these earthly creatures can bestow. Some snakes can be docile and as pets with good care and attention can become quite friendly companions. Thus, any creature who is mistreated or abused will react accordingly and snakes are no exception. So, my little creature friend and I had enjoyed many wonderful hours with her curled in my lap or feeling her cool earthy body slinking around my arms. Perhaps she was a unique personality because I am well aware of the fact that snakes are creatures of the wild. But my friend shared many a Full Moon and Sabbat Circle with my Coven. She represented to us a closeness to our ancient Mother Goddess. I looked into her eyes to see the wisdom of the ages and a reminder of our rebirth. Wrapped in her warmth I felt the embrace of Lilith surrounding me. We can all be empowered and inspired by recognizing the thread of one of the most powerful symbols of the Goddess.

There are multiple sources for research on the Goddess and her many personas. One of particular consequence is the "Encyclopedia Mythica" which interestingly does not list Lilith. So perhaps she was not just a story or myth but something much more real!

History and "herstory" are filled with dark tales of snakes, from the apple temptress to these desired but forbidden images of immorality, the Earth Mother Goddesses.

In mythology, Achelios was a Greek river god whose first form was a snake. He married the muse Melphomene and his daughters are the Sirens. The snake was the sacred creature of the Roman Goddess of good health, Hygieia. The Greek mythological Gorgon sisters named Steno, Euryole and Medusa, as well as Hecate were depicted with writhing snakes for hair. One of the oldest Goddess figures in Egypt, probably pre-dynastic was the Serpent Mother Iusaset, UA Zit, or Pr-Uatcher, known as the Celestial Serpent, giver of food and eternal life. Snakes thought of as the umbilical cord of life keep us threaded to the beginning.[2]

Another unique and not so known Serpent Goddess is Angitia.

Angitia (the Latin name of the Oscan Anagtia), is an Oscan healing and snake Goddess who was especially revered by the Marsi, a warlike tribe of people who lived to the east of Rome in the Apennine Mountains (sometimes called after them the Marsian Hills) and who spoke a Sabellan dialect. [...] Angitia was also associated with the Greek sorceress Kirke or Circe.[3]

Encyclopedia Mythica states that "she was a Roman snake-goddess who was especially worshipped by the Marsi, a tribe in central Italy." The Marsi were perhaps the original snake-charmers who channeled their Goddess Anagtia to aid them in charming snakes and curing their bites. The Marsi also celebrated the Feast of the Serpari (which is still held today) where snake charmers were held in great regard. It is also the feast of San Domenico on the first Thursday in May. He is a Saint who is recorded as having the ability to charm various snakes and send them away. Is that once again a synonym for hiding Lilith?

The Marsi's Goddess, Anagtia, was a healer who used her ability to save those who were poisoned, usually by snakes. "In Rome of the 1st century CE, the Marsi were reputed to be healers and fortune-tellers, and their land was considered a hotbed of witchcraft."[4]

Another fascinating Goddess who has almost been forgotten is Wadjet, one of the oldest known Goddesses. In Egyptian Mythology she was a Goddess of Justice, Time, Heaven and

Hell (also spelled Wadjit, Wedjet, Uadjet or Ua Zit and in Greek, Udjo, Uto, Edjo, and Buto among other names).

She was said to be the patron and protector of Lower Egypt and upon unification with Upper Egypt, the joint protector and patron of all of Egypt with the "goddess" of Upper Egypt. The image of Wadjet with the sun disk is called the uraeus, and it was the emblem on the crown of the rulers of Lower Egypt. She was also the protector of kings and of women in childbirth.

As the patron goddess, she was associated with the land and depicted as a snake-headed woman or a snake, usually an Egyptian cobra, a poisonous snake common to the region; sometimes she was depicted as a woman with two snake heads and, at other times, a snake with a woman's head. Her oracle was in the renowned temple in Per-Wadjet that was dedicated to her worship and gave the city its name. This oracle may have been the source for the oracular tradition that spread to Greece from Egypt.[5]

There are a number of Egyptian Serpent Goddesses that I find of interest. Almost lost to the ages, these powerful Goddesses of darkness need to morph back into our consciousness.

Kauket, the Goddess of Darkness, is a Goddess and female personification of darkness. She is part of the Ogdoad (a group of eight deities) and is depicted as a snake, or a snake-headed woman.

The Goddess Hauhet is the female personification of infinity or eternity.

Hauhet means ("endlessness") is part of the Ogdoad, she is usually depicted as a snake or snake-headed human. Her male counterpart is Heh (God of infinity and time).

Unut is a Snake Goddess. Unut ("The Swift One") (Wenut,

Wenet) was a snake Goddess from the 15th Nome of Upper Egypt and was worshipped with Thoth. In later periods she was depicted with a woman's body and a hare's head.[6]

As we discover the many serpentine Goddesses of antiquity we should also welcome the memories of their mortal Priestess counterparts. In honor of their Deities, these Priestesses became the best instrument with which to channel the essence of the Goddess. One after the other, ancient Priestesses danced in spiraling processions moving to freely choreographed aerobic phrases while banging tambourines, cills, rattles, flutes and sistrums. The dancers' ritual energy conjured up an atmosphere of joyous festivity and sacred Magick.

The Serpent Goddesses are the spiritual daughters of Lilith but as a Sacred Dancer, I see their Priestesses as being the earthly embodiment of Lilith's lasting momentum.

The spiraling dance of the Priestesses was and still is an integral part of spiritual celebrations. They spontaneously beat out the rhythm of Nature's pulse with their feet as their bodies wove the swirling patterns of the spiral procession. Now modern Sacred Dancers snake within and without to create their own hypnotic sacrament. Those of us who hold onto the ancient threads that bind us to the past still rejoice in the lively dances that honor the Serpent Goddesses.

Even now the Indonesian dancers display their intricate hand/finger movements as they mimic the swirling serpent in their movements. And the spiritually religious snake charmers whose movements intertwined with their earthbound creature performed their special Magick of healing, exorcism, obtaining fertility, protection and forgiveness.

Spiritual Daughters of the Goddess dancing in the flesh.

Endnotes

1.   https://en.wikipedia.org/wiki/Serpent_(symbolism)

2. Excerpted from - https://pantheon.org/search/?ie=utf-8&q=snake+goddesses
3. http://www.thaliatook.com/AMGG/angitia.php
4. http://www.thaliatook.com/AMGG/angitia.php
5. http://www.crystalinks.com/wadjet.html
6. Excerpted from - http://www.thewhitegoddess.co.uk/divinity_of_the_day/egyptian/unut.asp

Chapter 6

A Fable of Creation and Beyond ...

Mythologies abound and stories are re-told again and again. This is my version of the story of the birth of Lilith, Eve and Adam.

Once upon a time long before the world of reality and existence as we know it there was a Supreme Celestial Divinity. This Divinity was so awesome and powerful that it swirled around and encompassed every minute particle in an infinite panorama of self-created luminous lights and deep piercing darkness. Here Divinity began to create an eternal cosmos of unimaginable depth that was so miraculous that it began to erupt upon and within itself spewing forth a never-ending array of swirling fiery energy. Through the power and grace of Divinity's Supreme Being, consciousness emerged and particles of this energy began to form multi-faceted orbs. These orbs began to birth off into one unique cosmic display after another exploding into a boundless array of never ending stars and planets. Our vibrant and mysterious galaxy was born. Eternity stretched out into this mystifying display of intricate activity. As each bright orb became bolder and sought to be the brightest, in contrast each dark void pulled more blackness into itself. What began as a display of unsurpassed beauty slowly evolved into a cosmic puzzle of untold proportion and complexity. And Divinity watched and beheld the wonder of this vast creation.

The intricacy became so extreme yet so simple in its paradox that Divinity began to challenge realization within itself and began to form an interstellar inspiration. Divinity wished to mirror one tiny aspect of its own sacred wholeness into the conception of two halves. So, Divinity split apart the whole at the same time and thus created two small aspects of its Divine self. Equal halves with a unique consciousness born of Divinity's grace and love that fit back together like pieces of a puzzle. Thus, the cosmic experiment was begun. Lilith was birthed as the Yin fit within the birth of Adam as the Yang. Joined together in sacred wholeness they became a dynamic symmetry of sexual interaction. Lilith and Adam rising together from the hand of Divinity, therefore they were created equal. In Chinese medicine is it said of the Yin/Yang if one disappears, the other must disappear as well, leaving emptiness. Lilith and Adam created as mirror images yet opposing forces both interconnected and interdependent. These images became the female and the male with conscious thoughts of their own. Divinity watched and waited.

For as light balances dark, Divinity bestowed free will upon Lilith and Adam and thus all between them was meant to be given and taken evenly.

To enhance their existence, Divinity spun another intricate design in the creation of a garden of untold luxuriance and voluptuous abundance. Divinity called it the Garden of Eden, and surrounded Lilith and Adam in a paradise of living patterns and colors in the form of countless varieties of trees, plants and flowers. Lilith and Adam lived amongst foliage of unsurpassed splendor and plenty. And the birds flew above their heads in lovely colorful patterns. There were no unplanned or forbidden temptations within their garden, as all was within their grasp. Divinity had released Lilith and Adam to develop openly and freely.

Since all of their needs seemed to be met within this perfect environment, Lilith and Adam appeared happy. Yet Lilith, though content in her surroundings, craved more. Why would Divinity create free-thinking beings if not to encourage them to challenge their own thought processes? Lilith embraced her complexity and nurtured the evolution of her inner soul with its infinite appetite for more. She balanced her passionate and untamed sexuality with her strong motherly nature as she accepted the duality within herself. Adam although created equal to Lilith, also wished for more. Where Lilith expanded her mind, Adam expanded his physical strength. The scales of balance were tipping. Yet for all of his physical strength, Adam began to fear what he did not comprehend within Lilith. The more Lilith evolved, the more Adam's desire for her took control of his senses. Adam was in a quandary, for though mirror images of the Divine, they were still different. The balance was shifting and Adam wanted and needed to maintain control. Oblivious to Adam's concern, Lilith continued to develop in her own way. She was on a quest to understand her individual connection to the Divine within her soul. Divinity was intrigued and determined to allow these complex creations full rein to explore and learn from each other. Thus, the web of differences between these two creations was allowed to form and regretfully the whole became unstable.

The age-old dilemma of the power struggle between the sexes was born when Lilith declined most vehemently to lie beneath Adam in the act of copulation. The myth of a utopian paradise was shattered with one bold independent act and Divinity was challenged to its very core. But let us re-interpret Lilith's determination to remain equal and not succumb to a life on the bottom as a powerful moment in this ancient mythological story.

And from an equal sharing union, humanity could have sprung forth into a world of harmony and stability. Lilith and Adam should have brought us a Garden of Eden where peace, love and beauty reign amongst the vast lushness. So what changed the story and what tipped the balance? In my interpretation, Lilith does not fall from grace, instead she teaches Adam to control his fear and desires and to accept the differences between them. Each as a viable equal, both Adam and Lilith could experience each other in ways that complement their differences. Singular control does not play a part in my mythology. Instead their garden paradise grows to encompass a world where Divinity reigns supreme and sexual ecstasy defines balance.

Mine is a mythology whereby Lilith and Adam understand their genetic link to Divinity. Eve is born simply as a sister-half to Lilith instead of simply Adam's "wife." There is no subservience or guilt in my tale.

So, continuing my version of the myth, Eve born of necessity into a world of innocence tiptoed through the garden carefully. Instead of fearing the boundaries of free-thinking, she embraced knowledge and life. So, she danced swirling and twirling through the garden's lushness until she became fascinated with one particular tree. It not only graced her with its sumptuous fruit but its tantalizing wisdom. There was so much to learn and experience.

And if Divinity is the whole to which we mirror its two halves, then Divinity encompasses both the female and the male. Sacred Divinity must not be confined or defined by gender for such classification is beyond our scope as mere humans.

Sadly, the possibility of my happy mythology's ending drifted away millennia ago. We as humans, plus the world surrounding us became confused and we lost our way. The path to balanced ecstasy was hidden and all traces of the Garden dried up to bring forth the imbalance that we know and live today. The Sacred Divine was thrown away for more controllable singular god figures. These patriarchal identities disregarded the Sacred Feminine as Goddess and ruled, judged and shed blood in their God's name to maintain control and power. Just as any conscious thought of a Female/Male Divinity faded into nothingness so did the idea of a Sacred Divine within its purely feminine aspect.

For too long this strict dominance has controlled all facets of human development from religion to commerce. Women given the back door to all areas of worldly growth became the victims. Sadly, in time the victim succumbs willingly, knowing no other life than the one offered by their jailers. But roles reverse as the cosmos seeks to right the equilibrium and the suppressor becomes the suppressed as they wage battle after battle. Women's powers and their connection to the Sacred Feminine within themselves laid dormant for centuries upon centuries under this cloud.

Ah! Let the cosmic pendulum swing back and forth for in time it swings high enough to herald an awakening of the world's realization that Divinity lies within both female and male. Feminine seductive Lilith becomes just another aspect of the motherly nurturing Eve. Add Adam's male persona and we have completeness.

The Goddess as the Sacred Feminine of Divinity has made an astounding resurgence to right the balance. Our thoughts about our existence and the impact of ancient mythology has changed within this new era of scientific and spiritual growth. Though we are just at the first spark of dawn in our development, Lilith is beginning to emerge as the victorious first Woman with Eve taking her rightful place as first Sister. The time has come for women of every culture and race to shed the guilt brought down upon them by history and wholeheartedly welcome their link to the first sisters, Lilith and Eve. We are all sisters under the skin.

Thus, I must ascribe to Divinity as the Goddess in all Her Sacred Femininity not because I believe Divinity is only feminine, but because I seek this long-awaited balance. I wish I could really turn back the mythological clock and re-define the creation story. How different our world would be!

For too long Divinity had been thought of as just "God." With our new dawn we are finally reintroducing Divinity as the "Goddess." We are beginning to right the wrong. Only with this realization can female and male embrace the power and the awe of the Divine Feminine within each of us. We are ripe for understanding.

Chapter 7

Understanding Lilith and Eve as the Sacred Feminine through Meditation, Prayer, Invocation and Ritual

Part I: Into the Light

How does one go beyond herstory and history and begin to understand the Divine Feminine spark that is within each of us? This book seeks to play upon our destinies, transporting us into a balance of male and female that has been missing for so long. Our feminine and masculine personalities have been influenced by millennia of cultural mores that have sought to demoralize and bury the powerful feminine mystic. Yet the Divine Feminine as the Goddess has survived. She is within us and around us always. Her sacred presence has remained as simple and yet as intricate as the thin silken threads of a spider's web holding each of us fast within its grasp. Here is a threadlike memory that has traveled through time to bind mother to daughter again and again. Every culture no matter how patriarchal is bound to its mythologies by these memories.

Women are all sisters and we all come from the Divinity as Goddesses. Some whisper while others boldly call out her name. To me she is Lilith the first, Eve the second, Hecate the Wise, Selket the Healer and the great winged Isis whose longevity has traveled in the hearts of many people and that of Priestesses and Clergy like myself, even to this day.

Each Goddess persona is a reverent reminder of the power of the self, the feminine self. I call to every woman to awaken her inner feminine potency and learn to walk with the Goddess through relaxing meditation, empowerment rituals and sacred prayers and invocations. For the sanctified within the female and male touch reaches across all cultures and traditions.

Creating sacred space to welcome the Goddess within

Have you ever experienced a calming sensation upon entering a church or temple or walking through a quiet garden? It is this feeling that awakens the inner spirit and with focused awareness can grant one a moment of communion with the Divine.

Perhaps a possible explanation is the belief in Ley lines.

Leys or "Ley lines" are the grid patterns formed by drawing connecting lines between ancient megaliths, stone circles, and other ancient monuments. These monuments are said to mark the intersection of telluric energy currents (the natural electric currents that make up the earth's magnetic field). Many claim these areas are associated with increased paranormal activity or "gateways" for supernatural or inter-dimensional beings.[1]

It is a well-accepted fact that many ancient temples and churches were built in certain areas for a definite reason. Perhaps they sit atop the energy of Ley lines or ancient power spots known only to our ancestors, or mimic the night stars with their placement amongst other similar sites. Nonetheless, whenever I enter Trinity Church in lower Manhattan, which is one of the oldest buildings in downtown NYC, I can sense a cool calming energy permeate my being. Sitting in silent meditation in a pew brings me to a grounding place ... as if the earth beneath surrounds me in a Mother's embrace. Forgetting the Hollywood dogma of Templar treasure, the ground upon which this building was constructed does have an energy that goes beyond the patriarchal religious significance of the structure. I am not a member of the parish and I enter the building simply in my personal quest to find sacred spaces anywhere and everywhere. For my need to call upon the Goddess overtakes me anytime and anyplace. Buildings such as Trinity that are open to the public, can offer some moments' respite from a rather chaotic world. Each meditative moment with the Divine allows us to reach back in time to the Akashic genetic memories stored in all females and males. Let us continue to weave the thread of "herstory" that joins history and balances all reminiscences to each other.

Finding a private place for a brief or a long meditative moment with the Goddess doesn't have to be a challenge. Try a secluded area outdoors in a backyard or garden. Perhaps lying on the grass in a field or sitting on a rock near a stream; or even on a sandy beach. One can always just sit undisturbed on a couch or relax in a bed. Whatever the space, make it yours for meditation, however brief.

Meditate with Divinity

What is Meditation? "The act or process of meditating. A devotional exercise of or leading to contemplation. A contemplative discourse, usually on a religious or philosophical subject."[2]

I feel meditation encompasses a broad category that has a multitude of formats running the gamut from the deeply spiritual to simply relaxing and being reflective. It can also happen spontaneously. Have you ever walked down a wooded path during a nature walk deep in focused thought admiring the foliage or creatures scurrying about only to find that more time had passed than you had realized. Some would call it drifting or daydreaming, I call it spontaneous meditation with the Sacred Mother Earth as the Goddess. All you have to do is relax and clear your mind of any troublesome thoughts and take a few deep breaths. You will go into an "alpha" state of light meditation. You are totally conscious, but your brain waves are relaxed and you are in a neutral state. It definitely takes practice to clear one's mind by unwinding in this way. It is important to remember that in the beginning this should only be done in safe and private surroundings.

Another form of meditation is dance. It becomes a sacred ritual experience when you think of it as a reflection of the self. Let it be a profound expression of the soul. Performing dance meditation allows you to release tension and honor the moment. It can be highly athletic and complex to free-flowing and effortless. It can happen with formal preparation or simply spontaneously or a combination of both.

Think of the Mevlevi Order of Sufis, or Whirling Dervishes, as they are more commonly known, whose quest for spirituality culminates in a deep meditative state that is the result of using their bodies like spinning tops. Theirs is a form and practice of continuous, precise and much focused movements of the hands and feet. By extending their arms with the right palm facing up and the left palm down, they believe spiritual energy from above enters through the right palm, passing through the body and passing through the left palm and into the Earth. Though the Dervishes prepare for many hours before a ceremony, I see their deeply meditative trance as spontaneously and gloriously achieved when they begin their whirling movements.

Sacred, Mystical or Magickal dancing becomes the embodiment of a powerful inner motivation and inspirational meditation. It is the integration of the spirit to the mind which expresses the contemplative voice within. Thus, feeling the Spirit of the Goddess or God within through Sacred Movement and Dance can be the ultimate spiritual encounter with Divinity's essence.

The choreography of Isadora Duncan is another example of such sacred meditation through dance. Isadora wore her gossamer Grecian tunics and danced lyrical movements with her intense spiritual freedom. This spirit can still be seen today when dancers study and perform her graceful and sinuous choreography. The tradition of her natural choreographic style mimics the undulating waves and the soft breezes of the sea. It becomes the meditation within nature as movement for the soul.

Here we have meditation as a spiritual revelation of expression that allows for inner healing and a connection to the Divine within the context of dancing movement. Let it be your gateway to passion.

I would like to share an exercise in Sacred Meditative Dance that I have personally experienced and danced many times in my own garden. Wait for a clear moonlit night and experience this exercise in light reflective movement that I hope will inspire.

First take a ritual bath adding fragrant oils and herbs to the water and afterwards dress in comfortable loose clothing and soft shoes (or if possible naked and free). Then chose the right place, perhaps outside in a private garden or yard or a large room cleared of any obstructions and furniture. Let the Moon be at its fullest and the evening warm and clear. Scatter rose petals, or any flower petals that are available, around the (clean and level) sacred dance space that you have chosen. Before you begin, take a moment to relax your mind and spirit. You can either dance in silence with the sounds of nature for background or play any soft classical music that suits your mood.

With arms widespread to greet the Moon's bright orb say these words:

Great Goddess you are wise
You are grace itself
Like a dancer about to take flight

You beckon and I shall follow. Now begin to slowly spiral dance around the sacred space, letting your spontaneity build momentum with whatever dance movements come naturally, and free yourself to dance with the Goddess. (Move within a sense of your own level and creativity.) Feel the harmony and beauty of your movements as they become your own Divine Meditation. Let your spirit soar and let inspiration manifest through your body. Move at your own pace until you feel it is time to ground the energy you have created by touching the earth.

My special way of giving thanks is to blow a kiss to the Moon Goddess and then let that kiss also fall down to the earth.

This exercise could bring you closer to an intimate communion with Divinity if you allow yourself to be completely naked. Thus, the passionate energy of movement will enter your being unobstructed and unhampered by the restraints of clothing.

Meditation through movement is truly an experience with the Divine, and in that moment you can sometimes feel the passion of Lilith.

Meditation with Eve

On a sunny new moon morning indulge in a ritual bath with relaxing oils and herbs to sooth and cleanse away any stress. Change into comfortable clothing (in pastel colors) and bring a blanket and/or pillow to lie upon.

Find a safe and secluded area outdoors that can be your sacred space for this meditation. Perhaps lying on the grass in a field (or even your backyard); or sitting on a rock near a stream; or even on a sandy beach. Whatever the space, make it yours for this meditation.

Meditate on your back if possible facing the sky. Close your eyes and begin breathing deep relaxing breaths. Feel your body relax into the ground. Let your mind imagine youthful running, carefree in a lush garden paradise. See the flowers and smell their sweet fragrance. Look for your sister Eve who joins your mind in dancing abandonment. Feel the power she is capable of bringing to you. Do not feel her trepidation but her strong conviction. When you feel energized and free imagine taking the hand of Eve as the Goddess in yours and thank her and ask for her blessing. Then slowly bring yourself back to this world. Stretch out your limbs and open your eyes. Feel empowered.

Part II: Embracing the Darkness

Invoking Lilith through Meditation

Late night, preferably midnight, on a dark moon will bring you full circle with this meditative experience. As usual prepare yourself with a ritual bath. This time add soothing bath salts instead of oils and change into comfortable clothing (in dark earth or red tones) or once again naked if possible. Find a comfortable space either inside lying upon blankets and pillows on the floor or on the ground outside (anywhere that is secluded and completely safe and private). Once again relax your breath as you get comfortable and release any stress, tension or worries.

Close your eyes and imagine you are descending a spiral staircase into a dark cave. Walk carefully for there is no light. When you reach the bottom, visualize that you see light from numerous candles coming from a room at the center of the cave. There standing to greet you is a beautiful figure of a woman surrounded by the glowing flickering lights. She welcomes you with outstretched arms and whispers her name three times Lilith, Lilith, Lilith. Allow yourself to feel comfort in her embrace for she is the mother of all that is strength and passion within thee.

Visualize turning to her and putting your ear to her breath and listening ... for you will hear the words of wisdom. Then turn your face towards hers and thank her. Ask for her blessings of feminine empowerment and understanding. Accept from her hand a candle that you take back with you up the spiral staircase. Walk back up the spiral staircase higher and higher and let the bright candle flame light your way. Upon returning to the surface let the winds of change blow out the candle flame. Bury the candle within the earth as an offering. Allow yourself to slowly wake and come back into this earthly realm. Remember her gift to you ... the flame of knowledge and feminine power and above all desire. Stretch out your limbs and open your eyes.

Part III: Ritual Contemplation

Sacred Prayer

My definition of prayer is that it is simply a petition or supplication to Divinity by acts of praise and thanksgiving. In a graceful way, this application to the Divine can reward one with the knowledge that at the moment of reciting and beyond they are in union with the Sacred.

Evening Invocation to Lilith

Lilith, you are the absent Mother.
Passionate Muse of inspiration and achievement,
Ancient Sage of wisdom,
Let your worship ring forth through the ages.
Let your guidance infuse my dreams.
As your blessings light the path of my destiny.

Morning Invocation to Eve

Eve, you are the Maiden Mother.
Within your Blessings we are free
Of the yoke that befell us.
Help us to know ourselves
And to achieve our goals.

Prayer to Lilith and Eve

Sisters of Antiquity,
Bless me your Daughter with guidance.
Bless me your Sister with wisdom.
For I mirror your reflections
In the center of my soul.

Sacred Invocation

My interpretation of "invocation" is a brief ritual whereby the participant shows honor and reverence to a particular aspect/ persona of the Sacred Feminine as Goddess. Preparation is important. If you have an altar it should reflect whatever Deity's image you wish to honor. If you don't already have an altar you can substitute a small table or shelf. Add a vase of fresh flowers and a symbol or representation of the four elements, earth, air, fire and water. Perhaps you can add a small stone for earth, a feather for air, a lighted candle for fire, or a shell for water. On my altar to Lilith, I often add bird feathers that I've found on garden walks to represent her flight from bondage. Allow yourself to be creative in your interpretations.

Whenever possible take a ritual bath before any preparations are made. This will allow you a comforting few moments to soak away life's stress in water fragrant with herbs and/or oils.

Finding a comfortable area for you to create sacred space is also vital. I usually sweep my designated area with my sacred besom and burn sage or frankincense to cleanse the space of any unwanted energies. Then I find a comfortable seated position in front of my altar and allow myself to attune to my surroundings by listening for a bird's chirping or maybe the sound of the wind, or simply the sun's warmth from my window touching my skin. Briefly meditate to scan your chakra points and welcome balance and comfort to your inner being.

Let yourself feel the presence of your Deity and speak your words of "invocation."

(They can be read from words written in poetic form or just spoken spontaneously with the feelings of the moment.)

Invocation to Lilith and Eve

Great Goddesses of the Sacred Feminine, Lilith and Eve, Sisters of Antiquity, keepers of the flame of desire, truth and empowerment I honor you with my words. I ask for your blessing. It is with honor and reverence that I ask you to give me the strength and wisdom that I need this day for balance and to achieve my goals.

Continue the Invocation with these words:

Hail Lilith and Eve,
The Divine Light is within Thee.
Blessed are your restorative gifts of strength and healing.
Holy Mothers Ancient Goddesses of Hope
Let Your Sacred Essence spread among us now and forever.
So Mote It Be.

Balancing the Male persona within the Sacred Feminine

Let us visualize the ancient rites of Beltaine (May Day) when our female ancestors channeled Goddess energy and our male ancestors did likewise with God energy. This carnal union of Divinity on earth was achieved in equal measure. The Divine balance was believed to bring abundance and prosperity to all those who partook of its sensual pleasure.

Apollo, twin brother to Artemis, God and Goddess who shared balance at birth. Channeling the aspects of the three Muses, Apollo played his music on the lyre and recited his poetry. Apollo a revered God of substance acknowledged the symmetry of the male/female. Let his inspiration be yours.

Invocation for Men to gain understanding

God and Goddess, Yin and Yang. Divinity's pendulum swings back and forth. Great Goddess and God draw my spirit into balance. Let me contemplate the wisdom of unity. Let my God persona lead the way as my Goddess energy draws me deeper into the ecstasy of inner well-being. So Mote It Be.

Part IV: Finding Divine Wisdom in the Sacred Garden

A Dark Moon Ritual in honor of the first woman Lilith and her sister Eve

The name Lilith is said to derive from the Semitic word for night. Among her many mysterious traits she is said to rule over the spirits of the dead. The Indian translation of Eve's title "Mother of All Living" was a translation of Jaganmata, Kali Ma's Goddess of decay, death and rejuvenation. While Lilith guides the dead in their journey towards rebirth, her sister Eve brings forth the birth awakening. Together they rule the mysteries. Their combined energies can bring us closer to understanding and overcoming many of our inner fears. Lilith's bold energy can empower your independence and sexual confidence. While Eve's calm energy will empower your inner Madonna and nurturing persona. Together they create a balance of feminine energies. With a clear and deep acceptance of their complex myths, one can appreciate the extraordinary impact these fabled beings had on all women through the ages.

Why a dark moon ritual? Dark moon days are a time for inner reflection, strengthening spiritual growth and increasing psychic awareness. By channeling the energies of Lilith and/or Eve you can learn to open your mind and spirit to the Divine Feminine in all its mysterious and forgotten powers. This ritual is meant to deepen your understanding of meditation while developing your ability to commune with Divinity. Journey to the realm of the Sacred Garden and become one with these most ancient and misunderstood Goddess personas.

Plan to enact this ritual in the early evening of a dark moon night.

Ritual Preparation – Begin with the purification of Self: Indulge yourself in a ritual bath in flower scented water or burn incense of your choice or smudge yourself with the smoke of fragrant herbs.

Create your altar: Place your altar outdoors in a private garden or near a window in a quiet room facing towards the North direction (which symbolizes the element of the Earth – grounding and strength). Place upon your altar an image or statute of Lilith before a red candle to symbolize her rule over wanton passion and the potency of the mysterious unknown. Then place an image or statute of Eve before a white candle, symbolizing her persona of awakening and rebirth. Anoint each candle with Lotus oil (sacred Egyptian symbol and flower of the Goddess). Add a vase of exotic and colorful flowers to symbolize the Sacred Garden and an incense burner with your favorite incense.

Create the boundaries of your Sacred Garden: With a scattering of flower petals draw a circle around your altar, large enough to accommodate yourself comfortably. Light the incense.

Begin your ritual with an Invocation that calls forth the directions and further delineates your sacred space. Standing in front of your altar slowly move clockwise (beginning in the North and ending in the West) as you speak these invoking words:

I call forth the winds of life.

Cool breezes of the North bring to me the knowledge of the mysteries.

Fresh breezes of the East bring forth to me the dawn of knowledge.

Warm breezes of the South bring to me the knowledge of passion.

Sweet breezes of the West bring forth the Spirit of the Goddess.

In front of your altar say the words:

Lilith – fire and night,

Eve – fruit of life,
Honor me with your presence.
Light the red candle and say:
Lilith first of creation.
Light the white candle and say:
Eve first in creating.

Say these words as you light both the Lilith and Eve candles: I light these candles dark and light ... light and dark ... for without the night there can be no day ... the dark moon fades ... so that the new moon can ascend ... birth, life, death, and rebirth ... the circle never ends.

Now get into a comfortable sitting position. Take a moment to feel your entire body relax from your head to your toes. Inhale and exhale your breath calmly. Relax and try to clear your mind.

Close your eyes and begin to meditate upon the mysterious cycle of life and death. Envision flowers fading, leaves of trees turning vibrant oranges and gold, they are falling from the branches and scattering everywhere ... the world hovers in repose ... this is the dark moon time ... a potent time for deep inner reflection ... a time to build awareness of all that is around you ... a time to welcome the psychic senses. Stay here for a moment. Now imagine you are walking on the rich garden paths of the Sacred Garden that is not in repose any longer, but slowly awakening with each step you take ... and reflect upon the vast array of blossoming reborn flowers and plants. Imagine yourself rolling from side to side embracing the earth under you and feeling the fresh new petals titillate your skin and breathe deeply of their fragrance. Draw in their energies as you reflect upon your own inner needs. If you meet any animal and/or faerie totems along your path ... welcome them. Visualize the stars peeking out from the dark moon sky reflecting their sparkle all about the garden. Meditate upon these things.

Feel the flame of desire and passion inspire your spirit and feel the winds of change bring forth the power of the Divine Feminine. Open your senses to communion with Divinity.

In time (approximately 10–15 minutes) begin to stretch and slowly come back to this earthly realm. Take a moment to ground yourself by touching the cool earth (if you are outside). If you are inside, touch the floor and feel your energy penetrate deep down into the Earth Mother Gaia's earthly roots for balance. Slowly open your eyes.

Now standing before your altar – open your arms to receive and say:

Bless me dear Mother with love.
Bless me dear Sister with strength.
Bestow upon me your guidance
To inspire my soul
And to light my earthly path.

Walk around the perimeter of your circle counterclockwise three times in closing to release the forces that have been drawn to your ritual circle. Thank these energies who have graced you with their presence and bid them farewell.

Thank Lilith for her passionate vigor and Eve for her soft compassion. Snuff out the candles.

Gather up the petals that lined your sacred circle and bury them in your garden or add them to your burning incense.

So Mote It Be.

A little Spell to bring forth Sexual Empowerment:

To feel Lilith's energy wear red or scarlet for passion and courage.
To feel Eve's energy wear white for purity and healing.

Burn frankincense and say:

With the essence of the Goddesses Lilith and Eve surrounding my person

Be this my special spell to understand my hidden erotic desires.

Work your Magick well for me dear Sisters

This is my will. So Mote It Be!

Embrace yourself …

Blessed Be!

Endnotes

1. http://altreligion.about.com/library/glossary/bldefleys.htm
2. http://education.yahoo.com/reference/dictionary/entry/meditation

References

(The Bible King James Version with the Apocrypha, Penguin Press, Penguin Books, Ltd., 90 Strand London WC38 OR1, England).

Zohar (or Sefer ha-Zohar), 3ʳᵈ Edition, 1978, Wayne State University Press, Detroit, Michigan, USA

Book of Revelations Isaiah 34:14. from *Revelation and other Prophetic Books of the Bible*, St.

John the Evangelist and Others; 2016, 3ʳᵈ Edition, Dover Publications Inc. Mineola, NY, USA

Revelations, 12:14 (from New English Bible New Testament, 1961, Oxford University Press, Cambridge University Press).

Encyclopedia Mythica

https://pantheon.org/

The Alphabet of Ben Sira

http://jewishencyclopedia.com/articles/2888-ben-sira-alphabet-of Janet and Stewart Farrar, *The Witches' Goddess* by Janet and Stewart Farrar, 1984, Magickal Childe Publishing, NYC, USA

Greece, Rough Travel Guide, 9ᵗʰ Edition, May 5, 2015, Rough Guides

Raphael Patai, *The Hebrew Goddess*, (July 28, 2015), Ben Yehuda Press http://www.ecauldron.net/kabbalah.php

Dictionary.com Unabridged (v.1.1) Based on the Random House Unabridged Dictionary, c Random House Inc. 2006

Barbara Black Koltuv, Reprinted 1987, *The Book of Lilith*, Nicholas Hays, Inc.

http://altreligion.about.com/library/glossary/bldefsuccubus.htm

http://www.sria.org/lilith-the-demon/

http://altreligion.about.com/library/glossary/bldefsuccubus.htm

http://jewishchristianlit.com/Topics/Lilith/origin.html

(Kabbalah) Bacharach, 'Emeq haMelekh 23c-d; http://jewishchristianlit.com/Topics/Lilith/origin.html

https://en.wikipedia.org/wiki/Inanna

http://northernway.org/mmag.html (Mary Magdalene)

**(this website doesn't seem to exist anymore) but I did reference this site once in my book *Lilith as the Serpent* By Margi B. 2004-2005 on the LilithGate Website)

We think you will also enjoy…

Candle Magic, Lucya Starza

Using candles in simple spells, seasonal rituals and essential craft
techniques.

…a comprehensive guide on how to use candles for spells,
in rituals and for meditation and divination. It has quickly
become my preferred book for all aspects of candle magic.
Philip Heselton

978-1-78535-043-6 (Paperback)
978-1-78535-044-3 (e-book)

Celtic Chakras, Elen Sentier

Tread the British native shaman's path, explore the Goddess hidden in the ancient stories; walk the Celtic chakra spiral labyrinth.

Rich with personal vision, the book is an interesting exploration of wholeness.
Emma Restall Orr

978-1-78099-506-9 (paperback)
978-1-78099-507-6 (e-book)

Best Selling Pagan Portals & Shaman Pathways

Druid Shaman, Danu Forest

A practical guide to Celtic shamanism with exercises and techniques as well as traditional lore for exploring the Celtic Otherworld

A sound, practical introduction to a complex and wide-ranging subject.
Philip Shallcrass

978-1-78099-615-8 (paperback)
978-1-78099-616-5 (e-book)

Kitchen Witchcraft, Rachel Patterson
Take a glimpse at the workings of a Kitchen Witch and share in
the crafts

*A wonderful little book which will get anyone started on Kitchen
Witchery. Informative, and easy to follow.*
Janet Farrar & Gavin Bone

978-1-78099-843-5 (paperback)
978-1-78099-842-8 (e-book)

Moon Magic, Rachel Patterson
An introduction to working with the phases of the Moon

*...a delightful treasury of lore and spiritual musings that should be
essential to any planetary magic-worker's reading list.*
David Salisbury

978-1-78279-281-9 (paperback)
978-1-78279-282-6 (e-book)

Best Selling Pagan Portals & Shaman Pathways

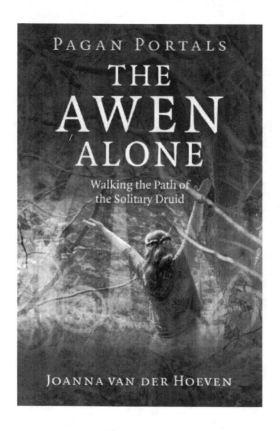

The Awen Alone, Joanna van der Hoeven
An introductory guide for the solitary Druid

Joanna's voice carries the impact and knowledge of the ancestors, combined with the wisdom of contemporary understanding.
Cat Treadwell

978-1-78279-547-6 (paperback)
978-1-78279-546-9 (e-book)

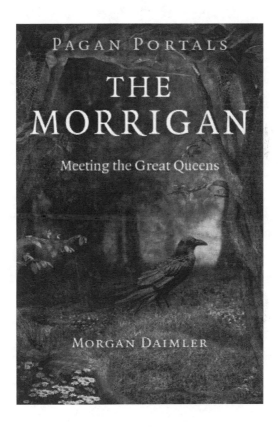

MOON
BOOKS

PAGANISM & SHAMANISM

What is Paganism? A religion, a spirituality, an alternative
belief system, nature worship? You can find support for all these
definitions (and many more) in dictionaries, encyclopaedias, and
text books of religion, but subscribe to any one and the truth will
evade you. Above all Paganism is a creative pursuit, an encounter
with reality, an exploration of meaning and an expression of the
soul. Druids, Heathens, Wiccans and others, all contribute their
insights and literary riches to the Pagan tradition. Moon Books
invites you to begin or to deepen your own encounter, right here,
right now.
If you have enjoyed this book, why not tell other readers by
posting a review on your preferred book site. Recent bestsellers
from Moon Books are:

Journey to the Dark Goddess
How to Return to Your Soul
Jane Meredith
Discover the powerful secrets of the Dark Goddess and
transform your depression, grief and pain into healing
and integration.
Paperback: 978-1-84694-677-6 ebook: 978-1-78099-223-5

Shamanic Reiki
Expanded Ways of Working with Universal Life Force Energy
Llyn Roberts, Robert Levy
Shamanism and Reiki are each powerful ways of healing; together,
their power multiplies. *Shamanic Reiki* introduces techniques to
help healers and Reiki practitioners tap ancient healing wisdom.
Paperback: 978-1-84694-037-8 ebook: 978-1-84694-650-9

Pagan Portals – The Awen Alone
Walking the Path of the Solitary Druid
Joanna van der Hoeven
An introductory guide for the solitary Druid, *The Awen Alone* will
accompany you as you explore, and seek out your own place
within the natural world.
Paperback: 978-1-78279-547-6 ebook: 978-1-78279-546-9

A Kitchen Witch's World of Magical Herbs & Plants
Rachel Patterson
A journey into the magical world of herbs and plants, filled with
magical uses, folklore, history and practical magic. By popular
writer, blogger and kitchen witch, Tansy Firedragon.
Paperback: 978-1-78279-621-3 ebook: 978-1-78279-620-6

Medicine for the Soul
The Complete Book of Shamanic Healing
Ross Heaven
All you will ever need to know about shamanic healing and how to
become your own shaman...
Paperback: 978-1-78099-419-2 ebook: 978-1-78099-420-8

Shaman Pathways – The Druid Shaman
Exploring the Celtic Otherworld
Danu Forest
A practical guide to Celtic shamanism with exercises and
techniques as well as traditional lore for exploring the Celtic
Otherworld.
Paperback: 978-1-78099-615-8 ebook: 978-1-78099-616-5

Traditional Witchcraft for the Woods and Forests
A Witch's Guide to the Woodland with Guided Meditations and
Pathworking
Melusine Draco
A Witch's guide to walking alone in the woods, with guided
meditations and pathworking.
Paperback: 978-1-84694-803-9 ebook: 978-1-84694-804-6

Wild Earth, Wild Soul
A Manual for an Ecstatic Culture
Bill Pfeiffer
Imagine a nature-based culture so alive and so connected,
spreading like wildfire. This book is the first flame...
Paperback: 978-1-78099-187-0 ebook: 978-1-78099-188-7

Naming the Goddess
Trevor Greenfield
Naming the Goddess is written by over eighty adherents and
scholars of Goddess and Goddess Spirituality.
Paperback: 978-1-78279-476-9 ebook: 978-1-78279-475-2

Shapeshifting into Higher Consciousness
Heal and Transform Yourself and Our World with Ancient
Shamanic and Modern Methods
Llyn Roberts
Ancient and modern methods that you can use every day to
transform yourself and make a positive difference in the world.
Paperback: 978-1-84694-843-5 ebook: 978-1-84694-844-2

Readers of ebooks can buy or view any of these bestsellers by
clicking on the live link in the title. Most titles are published in
paperback and as an ebook. Paperbacks are available in traditional
bookshops. Both print and ebook formats are available online.

Find more titles and sign up to our readers' newsletter at
http://www.johnhuntpublishing.com/paganism
Follow us on Facebook at https://www.facebook.com/MoonBooks
and Twitter at https://twitter.com/MoonBooksJHP